LIPS

CW00864869

LIBRARY BOOKS

The Story of Boots

Booklovers Library

JACKIE WINTER

Chantries Press
DORSET, UK

Chantries Press, Dorset, UK

Book Layout ©2016 Createspace.com and Chantries Press

Cover Image Dudley Store 1953, courtesy of The Boots Company PLC

Lipsticks and Library Books . 1st ed.

ISBN-13: 978-1535512589

ISBN-10: 153551258X

For Pat,
thank you for all your help and encouragement

Table of Contents

1. HALF A MILLION SUBURBAN HOUSEWIVES BECOME BOOTS BOOKLOVERS

"Laura Jesson is sitting at the downstage table having tea. She looks exactly what she is, a pleasant ordinary woman, rather pale for she is not very strong and with the definite charm of personality which comes from natural kindliness, humour and a reasonable conscience. She is reading a Boots library book at which she occasionally smiles. On the chair beside her, there are several parcels as she has been shopping."

From "Still Life" Noel Coward 1936

Madam, a circulating library in a town is an evergreen tree of diabolical knowledge! It blossoms throughout the year and depend on it, they who are so fond of handling the leaves, will long for the fruit at last.

This was Sheridan's opinion, expressed in his play "The Rivals", first performed at Covent Garden in 1775. He had good reason to issue dire warnings about the danger of novels possessing a low moral tone. 1748 had seen the publication of "Memoirs of a Woman of Pleasure", otherwise known as "Fanny Hill". John Cleland wrote this, while serving time in a debtors' prison in London. Not long after publication, the author found himself in court once again, charged with: "Corrupting the King's subjects." His novel became one of the most prosecuted and banned books of all time.

At the beginning of the 19th century there were about a thousand circulating libraries in the country and as Sheridan had feared, they enjoyed an unsavoury reputation for supplying vulgar and sordid novels. Amongst these was a highly controversial book, written by Charlotte Dacre in 1806, entitled "The Moor" or "Zofloya". This provoked outraged condemnation, due to its explicit content of neurotic obsessions, sadistic passions, sexual transgressions, supernatural terrors and eternal damnation: *"Her mind, alas, was an eternal night, which the broad beam of virtue never illuminated."*

Thirty years later Queen Victoria ascended the throne and doubtless there were many books of which she disapproved. But the queen enjoyed reading, especially novels by Marie Corelli, best selling writer of melodramatic gothic romance. A review in the Spectator described this writer as: *"a woman of deplorable talent who imagined that she was a genius."*

In 1842, Queen Victoria became the first British reigning monarch to travel by train - all the way from Slough to Paddington. In that same year Pentonville prison was built and an Act of Parliament prohibited women and children under ten from working in coalmines.

It was against this backdrop that Mudie's Select Library opened in Bloomsbury, on 10th June 1842. It was an enterprise that proceeded to dominate the literary scene throughout most of the Victorian era and transform the circulating library into a respectable institution.

Charles Edward Mudie set high standards and no books of low moral taste were permitted to violate his respectable shelves. W.H. Smith's circulating libraries entered the arena in 1860 and for the following forty years, these two giants had the world of the subscription library pretty much sewn up.

Then, as the century ebbed away, Jesse and Florence Boot made a momentous decision to open libraries in both their Nottingham chemist's shops and very soon Mudie's and Smith's realised they were facing formidable competition.

With attractive and comfortable surroundings, clean books, relatively affordable subscriptions and the lure of a tempting in-store cafe, Boots library was hard to resist. A pleasant morning could be spent choosing books, followed by chatting with friends over coffee and dainty fruit scones, at pleasant tables adorned with hand embroidered table cloths.

Boots' subscribers were essentially middle class and predominately women. During the 1920s only about 25% of library users were men. In its publicity material the company would portray their typical library user as an elegantly made up young woman, with fashionably styled hair. In reality, customers probably tended to be comfortably off married women, spanning early middle age to those of advanced years.

In the early 20th century it was often a woman's responsibility to choose books for the whole family. The man of the house might well enjoy reading "The Hound of the Baskervilles" by Arthur Conan Doyle, whilst possibly looking askance at his wife absorbed in "Sons and Lovers", one of D.H. Lawrence's most highly acclaimed novels. Popular books for girls at this time included "Anne of Green Gables" by L.M. Montgomery, while a young lad would certainly have preferred Kipling's "Just So Stories."

Class distinction dictated even the type of circulating library to which a woman belonged.

Virginia Woolf did not patronise Boots but went to Mudie's or to Day's, a select London library. In Volume One of her diaries she wrote scornfully of the women she saw there.

"Day's at 4 in the afternoon is the haunt of fashionable ladies, who want to be told what to read. A more despicable set of creatures I never saw. They come in furred like seals and scented like civets, condescend to pull a few novels about on the counter and then demand languidly whether there is <u>anything</u> amusing."

Boots was a far more broadly based library, catering as much for suburban shoppers as for stylish ladies. However, Florence Boot understood the importance of providing a comfortable and sumptuous environment for the affluent clientele she hoped to attract.

The libraries quickly flourished during the interwar years. By 1920 there were 500,000 subscribers and by 1938 books were being exchanged at the rate of 35 million each year. Romances and detective fiction were especially popular.

Jo Blackwell, a junior subscriber, remembers going to her library in St Agnes on Sea as a child and being very impressed by the sweeping staircase leading up into the library.

"My mother bought me a "Books I have Read" book," Jo recalls. "I was a quick and avid reader and the Boots librarian let Mum bring lots of books home for me. I loved Enid Blyton and also Laura Lee Hope's "Bobbsey Twins" stories."

John Burrows became a young subscriber at Boots' Skegness branch, in the late 1940's.

"My mum backed my application for a ticket," he remembers. "I felt very proud, walking into the children's section for the first time. I enjoyed all the Biggles books by W.E. Johns. Other favourite writers were Percy F. Westerman and Commander Sir Stephen King-Hall."

During the pre-war years, the free public libraries were thought to be unsuitable places for women and especially for well brought up young girls. They were generally considered dubious institutions, frequented by the lower classes, with an unpleasant whiff of charity about them and where the books were probably infested with nasty diseases.

Ruth Hunt was a young subscriber in Derby during the late 1940's. "My mother was rather a snob and she encouraged me to use Boots," Ruth says. "She was afraid that books from the public library might be full of germs."

People had a very real terror of disease at this time. In the 1950s there were 45,000 cases of polio in the UK and hundreds died. In 1957 an outbreak of Asian flu engulfed the world, resulting in over two million deaths.

Boots understood their subscribers' fears and took a firm stance on cleanliness. Their promotional literature stressed the importance attached to hygiene.

*"Every effort is made by the Management to safeguard subscribers from risk of infection. Where Library books are known or suspected to have been in infected areas, they are immediately destroyed **By Fire**."*

For housewives bored with tedious routine, a visit to the library provided a welcome escape. The heroine of Noel Coward's play" Still Life", was one such woman.

Laura Jesson is sitting at the downstage table having tea. She looks exactly what she is, a pleasant ordinary woman, rather pale for she is not very strong and with the definite charm of personality which comes from natural kindliness, humour and a reasonable conscience. She is reading a Boots library book at which she occasionally smiles. On the chair beside her, there are several parcels as she has been shopping.

"Still Life" is better known to most as the film version "Brief Encounter" (1945) in which Celia Johnson plays Laura Jesson. Elsie Matthews worked as a library assistant at the Stockton-On-Tees branch during the 1940s. "I remember the staff being called together for a special meeting and told about a new film called "Brief Encounter", Elsie says. "Boots libraries featured in the film and we were all encouraged to go and see it. Everyone was very excited."

Laura - the heroine of "Brief Encounter", was clearly on good terms with the librarian at her branch of Boots. *"Miss Lewis had at last managed to get the new Kate O'Brien for me. I believe she'd kept it hidden under the counter for two days."* This shows how popular Kate O'Brien was in the 1940s. The book Laura was so eager to read would probably have been "The Last of Summer" published in 1943, a love story set in prewar Ireland and tinged with mystery and tragedy.

During the Second World War the number of library subscribers increased to one million and Boots were buying 1,250,000 books each year. This gave the company considerable influence in the world of publishing.

Boots often advertised intriguing new titles: *"That book of memoirs which has aroused so much controversy. Those racy letters you heard about on the radio."* In 1950 one of these books would almost certainly have been the best selling   "Little Princesses: The Story of the Queen's Childhood by her Nanny". This was written by Marion Crawford, governess to the young Elizabeth and Margaret Rose.

The Royal family and especially the Queen Mother were furious at what they perceived as a betrayal of trust. They never forgave Crawfie - as the princesses called her and she was shunned by the Royals and their immediate circle for the rest of her life.

Public appetite for royal scandal was further stimulated in 1951 with the publication of "A King's Story: memoirs of the Duke of Windsor." Although fifteen years had passed since the abdication, a doomed love story never fails to fascinate.

In 1956, it was the woman's turn to tell all. "The Heart has its Reasons: the memoirs of the Duchess of Windsor" was published in 1956 but seemingly not to general acclaim. The Saturday Review on October 6th 1956 was scornful: *"In her memoirs, Wallis has made herself a faceless, emotionless, personality-less woman, who remembers almost everything that went on around her but nothing about herself."*

Boots libraries are certain to have stocked multiple copies of these books about the Royal family and of the Coronation in 1952. They were reviewed in the press and given wide publicity so subscribers would have been keen to read them.

Love stories, whether concerning the Queen's family or a more humble one, have always fascinated readers. Mavis Archer worked as a library assistant at the Nottingham branch from 1952 - 1962 and remembers many middle aged and elderly subscribers, who were Mills and Boon fans.

"They would come in most mornings," Mavis recalls, "settle themselves in a comfy chair and read for an hour or so. Then they'd go to Boots' cafe for a cup of tea and a buttered scone, before returning to the library and finishing their light romance."

Many older women had never worked, or left work when they married. Even Boots - a fairly enlightened employer - required a woman to resign as soon as the wedding ring was on her finger. It suited husbands to assume their wives found fulfilment in domestic duties, never thinking that housebound life could be monotonous and dull. These were the days before nights out with the girls, hen parties,

Pilates or reading groups. "A visit to the library played a big part in those women's lives," Mavis says.

Ruth Hunt remembers the attractive restaurant adjoining her Boots library in Derby. When Ruth was about fourteen she was allowed to meet her friends there, after choosing her library books.

"This made me feel very grown up." Ruth looks reflective. "It was probably my first venture into independence."

Elizabeth Mooney often went with her mother to Boots library, after a visit to Harrods.

"The library was on the second floor," Elizabeth recalls. "From an early age I loved everything about it - not just the shelves of enticing books but the exciting covers, the feel of the pages and the attractive drawings and photographs."

When she was fifteen years old, Janet Johnson began work with a small firm in Leicester. She remembers one of the firm's partners buying her a Boots subscription as a birthday gift.

"He knew how much I enjoyed reading and wanted to encourage me," Janet says. "It was quite something in 1953, for a teenager to belong to Boots library. I felt quite posh, walking through those doors."

As a sixteen-year-old girl, it was Ruth Fiander's ambition to belong to Boots library in Bournemouth.

"I took my school certificate in 1949 and vowed that if I passed, I would treat myself to a year's subscription." Ruth smiles. "When I found out I'd passed the exam, the first thing I did was join Boots library."

Paddy Blackburn's family lived in an outlying village some miles from Bradford. When Paddy was thirteen she was allowed to take the bus into the city all by herself, to change her mother's library books.

"I felt very brave and grown up," Paddy remembers. "Mum used to mark up the latest Boots' catalogue with a selection of titles she fancied. I enjoyed the bus journey home even more when I'd found some books I knew she wanted to read."

The young Paddy was happy to search the shelves for books but many subscribers preferred library assistants to do the legwork. Staff knew they were expected to make every effort to please customers, especially those who subscribed to the "On Demand" service which guaranteed the supply of any book within three days, always provided the title was in print. In 1926 that particular subscription cost a whopping 42 shillings a year.

This was a pricey indulgence, considering the annual wage of a male factory worker in 1925 was a little over £200, while his female equivalent was paid less than half that amount.

Class A subscribers paid an annual 17s 6d for the privilege of choosing any book on the shelves, regardless of popularity or date of publication. By far the greatest number of subscribers fell into the Class B bracket, which cost 10s 6d but they were restricted to borrowing books which were over a year old.

On joining, Class A subscribers were given a notebook, in which they wrote their preferences or specific books they wished to read and this was kept at the library. On each visit, borrowers expected to be greeted by name and given individual attention. They would make themselves comfortable, while a library assistant found their personal notebook and began to scour the shelves in search of an acceptable book. They could have more than one at a time but this entailed an extra charge, depending on how long they kept the book.

All Boots' books had the distinctive Green Shield embossed on their covers. There were eyelet holes at the top of the spines, into which a tag was inserted when the book was borrowed - green tag for first class subscribers and red for second class.

Boots had subscribers living abroad who made use of their postal service. This was proudly proclaimed in a staff magazine called The Bee in 1925:

"The little green label must be something like the British flag. It floats (or is distributed) over the entire English-speaking world. There appears to have been a boom lately in "Friends Abroad" subscriptions in Kenya Colony. Obviously the first satisfied subscriber conveyed his satisfaction to his next door neighbour - if one has a next door neighbour in Kenya Colony!"

Terry Kelly's mother worked as a cleaner for Boots at St Peter's Street in Derby. She had a staff discount for the store but Terry isn't sure if that entitled her to reduced library subscription rates. Terry didn't read much fiction so found the selection limiting.

"But I often had a bit of luck at sale time." He smiles. "Once I found a book by Terence Robertson, called "The Ship with Two Captains", a factual account of the part played by HMS

Seraph in WW2. I still have that in my collection, complete with its green shield."

Boots had regular book sales, mainly to dispose of stock that was no longer in pristine condition. Sometimes multiple copies of very popular books were bought, in order to fulfil initial demand quickly. But once early enthusiasm had subsided, it didn't look good to have too many copies of the same title languishing on the shelves.

Boots advertised sales ahead of time in the Quarterly Guides, which were made available to subscribers. These guides gave details of new and popular books which had recently been added to stock and ones which had become surplus to requirements.

"A limited number of copies of the works mentioned herewith will ultimately become available for sale at the prices quoted. Orders will be accepted for any of the volumes listed and supplied at the earliest possible moment."

Book sales provided excellent value for money. Margery Allingham's detective story entitled "The Fashion in Shrouds" is listed in a 1939 Quarterly Guide as being reduced from 8s 6d to 2s 6d. "A Blunt Instrument" by Georgette Heyer had the same reduction in price.

John Bolt purchased Boots books second hand in Oxford. He recalls the pleasure he felt - as a penniless youth - when given the chance to buy titles so cheaply. He was especially thrilled when he found anything connected to aviation.

"I still have six," he says. "Five are rebound in plain cloth covers of red, blue or green and the other is still in its original binding. Each has the distinctive metal eyelet at the top of the spine and the little green shield on the front cover." John has always regretted arriving late at the library on the day it finally closed. "All my favourite books on aviation had gone. I was so disappointed."

Book sales were obviously appreciated by a great many less affluent readers. This was pointed out in a letter to the Times Literary Supplement from E.G. Collieu at Brasenose College Oxford in February 1966:

"On the day when the last Boots branch closes, I write to draw attention to one particular service which it, like other subscription libraries now defunct, performed... viz. the ex-libris sales. Two generations must recall, with something more than nostalgia, the arrival every few months of the Catalogue of Bargains which - if the order was despatched by return of post - never failed to produce a rich haul of much needed and valuable books, for a few shillings the lot. In this way, the library not only satisfied numberless casual readers but also enabled many like myself, when an impecunious under graduate in the 1930's, to lay the foundations of a serious library otherwise unattainable."

This letter indicates that a substantial amount of the book stock was far from frivolous in content. Yet it would seem that Boots catered predominantly for women and provided mostly novels. As late as 1951, an article in the Economist suggested why people turned to circulating libraries.

"In even the biggest and most liberally provided public library, the addict of one class of novel - be it typist marries boss or riding the range - can only find enough of them to whet his appetite. The selection is too wide and the turnover too slow to provide a feast of any one style and the

reader must soon either broaden his tastes or indulge his passion in a circulating library."

It was also in 1951 that Rowntree and Lavers conducted a social history of reading habits, which confirmed that fiction was the mainstay of Boots and W.H. Smith's. Of the 50,000,000 volumes issued each year, non-fiction accounted for only around 10% and almost three quarters of subscribers were women.

Novels intended for a female readership between the wars, were generally written by middle class women for middle class women. Aided by new labour saving devices such as vacuum cleaners and fridges, the reasonably affluent housewife had more leisure time to enjoy reading, hence soaring subscriptions to Boots libraries. This was the heyday of fiction written by women, sadly due in part to the untimely death in both World Wars of many potential male novelists.

Former library assistants have occasionally expressed surprise at the appetite for light fiction, demonstrated by their grandest and wealthiest customers. Most class A subscribers seemed content to sit and wait, while a member of staff hunted down the latest love stories. The indulged upper classes, accustomed to being looked after in every area of their lives, could confidently expect to be spoilt during a trip to Boots library.

Carol Worral recalls a high-ranking police officer, who borrowed a thriller every day from the Boots library in Leicester, where she worked. Sir Robert Mark served as Chief Constable of Leicester City Police and later as Commissioner of the Metropolitan Police. His father was horrified when Robert chose his career, suggesting that it was only one step better than going to prison.

Many subscribers liked to keep their own record of books they'd read, with favourable or disparaging comments. Pat Oldale, who worked in several Bournemouth branches in the 1960s, remembers a subscriber called Captain Battle, a retired sea captain who was reputed to have captained the Queen Mary.

"Each time he came in, he produced a thick notebook which he called his bible," Pat told me. "He wrote down every title as he read it, with appropriate comments. One of his favourites was NBG."

Rachel Cory and her husband were visiting Blenheim Palace in 1958 when they glimpsed the Duke of Marlborough walking across the courtyard, with a book tucked under his arm.

"We knew it was from Boots library because my husband spotted the Little Green Shield," Mrs Cory said. "But we couldn't see the title of the book. Most disappointing!"

2. FLORENCE BOOT - LIBRARY LADY

"My earliest recollections are of toddling round the counters at my father's side and learning from him that all labour was dignified and that to be courteous and obliging was a great asset in the business world and that life in a shop could and ought to be a high calling."

Florence Boot, 1913.

Florence Annie Rowe was born in St Helier in 1863, the second daughter of William Rowe, a successful bookseller and stationer. Florence was 23 years old when she met Jesse Boot. He was a dozen years her senior and after spending practically every hour of the previous two decades building up his business, most probably looked even older. The Nottingham entrepreneur was on holiday in Jersey, recovering from a total physical breakdown.

A complete novice when it came to chatting up pretty young women, Jesse was immediately captivated by the attractive, vivacious Florence. After a short and romantic courtship, the engagement ring was barely on her finger before the couple were married by special licence in St Helier on 30th August 1886.

His wife's extrovert personality probably halted Jesse's premature decline into exhausted middle age and certainly rejuvenated his passion for the business. Florence was as enthusiastic and motivated as Jesse and her flair for fashion and design launched a new flow of ideas, putting women at the forefront of progress.

Florence had been brought up in the retail trade and had sound business sense. Jesse's respect for his wife rapidly increased and very soon he launched the Number 2 department within his Nottingham store, putting Florence in sole charge. The chemist's business remained as Number 1 department, a distinction that continued for many years.

Florence was described by one of her senior employees as being:

"Without doubt, responsible for the commencement and development of the fancy and toilet department. A somewhat masterful lady of striking appearance and as Mr Boot once rightly remarked to me "a woman of very good taste".

Believing that women should have beautiful things to look at while waiting for their medicines to be made up, young Mrs Boot filled the shelves with books, fancy goods, artists' materials, picture frames and gift ideas for every occasion.

When Jesse opened his second store in Nottingham his wife's artistic flare was evident throughout. There were entire departments for toiletries, books, stationery and perfumes, all displayed on quality mahogany counters.

Above the ground floor there was an ornate gallery, supported by a colonnade of cast-iron pillars, where pictures - all personally chosen by Florence - were hung in artistic arrangements. Attractive displays of decorative glass and silverware tempted awestruck customers.

This shop showcased Florence's artistic skill and original thinking and was to become the model for future Boots department stores across the country. Husband and wife worked together, planning every detail of new shop facades, interior fittings and decoration. Each store was designed to be a local landmark, where shopping would not be a chore but an enjoyable experience.

By 1893, Jesse and Florence had opened 33 Boots chemist's shops in the UK. At the turn of the century this number had grown to more than 250 and comprised a retail chain that far outstripped any rival.

The libraries were a natural progression from selling books. They began on a very modest scale, when Florence bought a stock of second hand titles from big London libraries. She placed these in revolving bookcases in about a dozen chemist shops and implemented a simple scheme for lending them to customers.

Boots fledgling library provoked the curiosity of a clever and ambitious young man named Mercer Stretch, who worked for Mudie's Subscription Library in London. Intrigued by the number of books being purchased by Florence, he decided to find out what she was up to.

Young Mrs Boot was doubtless very taken with the energetic fellow who cycled all the way from London to Nottingham, expressly to meet her. Impressed by

Florence's ideas, Mercer Stretch saw huge potential for growth and in 1899 he accepted the offer of a position as Boots' first Head Librarian. Under his charismatic leadership, Boots Booklovers Library began to expand and succeed at a rapid pace.

Florence's plan to combine a library with a chemist's shop was an immediate success. A mixture of shrewd judgement and simple common sense combined to make the new project a major asset to the company. Florence wanted her libraries to encourage customers into the shops, to borrow books but also to be side tracked into making purchases.

So libraries were always positioned either at the back of stores or upstairs, giving subscribers ample opportunity to be tempted by the enticing range of goods on display. Such was their popularity that libraries soon began to appear in many of the larger stores. Nottingham was followed by Lincoln and then Sheffield, Rotherham, Grantham and Cambridge. In fewer than ten years, Boots Booklovers were making themselves at home in 200 of the 371 shops.

Mercer Stretch and Florence devised a system of circulating the stock, thus enabling subscribers to borrow a book from one branch and return it to any other they chose. This ease of access helped to encourage commuters, holidaymakers and commercial travellers.

Jesse Boot envisaged the libraries as being *"extensively patronised by a thoughtful and cultured circle of customers"*, so quality and comfort were top of the list. This was exactly the sort of challenge that appealed to Florence and she set herself the task of supplying a luxurious environment and unparalleled customer service.

Boots libraries were designed to emulate the style of a comfortable country house and endeavoured to imitate the aristocratic refinement of a gentleman's private study. A great deal of thought was given to interior design. Its primary function was to eliminate any disagreeable thoughts connected to the immediate vicinity of a chemist's shop.

Everything possible was done to provide the subscriber with a warm and pleasant experience. Clean and carefully selected books were arranged on mahogany shelves, which were conscientiously dusted each morning by junior staff. There were heavy brocade curtains, cosy rugs and parquet flooring, partially covered with thick carpets.

The colour scheme seems to have scorned practical considerations, since Plymouth library was carpeted in cream and gold and Derby boasted Copenhagen Blue. Subtle shades were used for soft furnishings and sometimes for the woodwork.

Comfortable velvet sofas were positioned alongside coffee tables, on which lay sheets of creamy writing paper and beautifully arranged vases of flowers, often brought in by staff from their own gardens.

The latest copies of fashionable periodicals were always available. "Queen" magazine was popular at the time, focusing as it did on British High Society and the lives of the aristocracy. "The Lady", Britain's oldest weekly women's magazine, has always been a favourite, offering its own distinctive advice on topics such as beauty, etiquette and fashion. An issue dated 11th November 1909 contained this stern warning: *"A well dressed woman produces a pleasant effect according to the degree and perfection of her taste*

*but the over-dressed woman produces an effect as
repugnant, if not obnoxious."*

Boots employed a London architect named Morley Horder
to design statues, heraldic devices and stained glass, to
decorate their new buildings. Florence ensured that her
libraries were primary recipients of these features. Picture
windows, inlaid with beautiful stained glass, invariably
provided views across a neighbouring market square or
high street. Library design focused on meeting middle class
notions concerning desirable surroundings.

However, Florence aimed to offer subscribers far more than
an agreeable environment. Librarians were carefully trained
to serve customers and the newest titles could always be
found on the shelves. Customers were permitted - if not
exactly encouraged - to chat to friends in the library, which
was consequently not an entirely silent space.

In 1900, virtually all vehicles in busy cities were horse
drawn. Upper class people of wealth and social position,
who were rich enough to keep their own carriages and
could afford stabling for horses, were dubbed "carriage
trade". These prosperous folk usually patronised the long
established, and well regarded, Mudie's circulating library.

Although Florence would have been pleased to lure a few
affluent customers away from Mudie's, she really intended
her libraries to appeal to the comfortably off middle class.
Consequently, Boots subscription rates were carefully set a
little lower than Mudie's.

In1901, membership cost 10s 6d a year for one volume at a
time, 16s 6d for two, 21s for three, 42s for six and 7s for
each additional volume. On joining, subscribers were issued

with a membership token, which also served as a bookmark.

At the turn of the century, the annual wage for a general labourer was £68, whereas a teacher could expect to earn £147.   So Boots library was well within reach of the expanding middle class.

In the earliest catalogue of books, Guernsey could be found among the thirteen branches offering a library service and this reflected Florence's loyalty to the Channel Islands and her Jersey roots. Most of the other branches were in the Midlands but the seaside town of Weymouth, the port for steamers bound for Jersey and Guernsey, also had a branch within its chemist's shop.

In 1903, Mercer Stretch produced a clothbound five hundred-page catalogue, priced at one shilling. Fiction predominated and brief plot outlines of the books were provided. Following on from the success of this catalogue, a second was issued in 1905. This was more substantial, headed up with a photograph of the Brighton branch library, a modern and elegant building, designed to appeal to middle class taste and expectations.

This new catalogue contained works of history, biography and travel, as well as a long list of fiction titles. There was also a much shorter section devoted to children's books. In Jesse Boot's preface, he commended the cleanliness of the stock and the magnificently fitted and well equipped libraries.

The star attraction of the periodical list produced in 1919 was three volumes of the "Life and Letters of Queen Victoria", offered for sale at five shillings for the set. *"These copies have been withdrawn from circulation and are guaranteed in FINE FRESH CONDITION."* Amongst Popular Authors And Their Latest Works listed in the 1919 catalogue were new books by Rider Haggard, Arthur Conan Doyle, Arnold Bennett, Ethel M Dell, Baroness Orczy and Mrs Humphrey Ward.

Also included was a novel entitled "The Years for Rachel", by Berta Ruck, whose married name was Mrs Oliver Onions. A prolific writer, Berta Ruck produced four titles in 1918 alone and over the course of 67 years she wrote ninety romantic novels. A review in the Spectator on 12th October 1918 spoke scathingly of "The Years for Rachel." *"A story of a very long engagement, of which the reader will get almost as tired as did the heroine."*

On page six of the Library Regulations in the 1919 catalogue, Sir Jesse Boot made a specific contribution in his role as MD of Boots Booklovers Library. *"It is drawn to the attention of subscribers that the Managing Director reserves the right to withhold from circulation or withdraw from stock, any book, for whatever cause he may think desirable."*

Jesse had high moral standards, which he chose to believe were shared by subscribers. However, aware of a responsibility to satisfy the literary requirements of a vast number of paying customers, Jesse was obliged to allow shelf space for the occasional book which doubtless earned his disapproval.

One of these may well have been "The Sheik" written by E.M. Hull in 1919, a lurid tale of a young girl kidnapped by an Arab Sheik and held captive in his tent. Fortunately, the sadistic brute eventually transformed into a thoroughly decent English chap, with a plausible explanation for his unpleasant behaviour.

"The Sheik" quickly became an international blockbuster, selling over 1.2 million copies worldwide. Its popularity was enhanced in 1921, when Rudolph Valentino starred in a film version of the book, establishing his reputation as the greatest lover of the silent screen.

Rudolph Valentino died on August 23rd 1926, of complications after surgery for appendicitis. He was only thirty-one. On the day of his funeral an estimated 10,000 people lined the streets of New York. Some devastated fans committed suicide.

The library initiative took its place amongst other forays into expansion, spearheaded by Florence. One of these was the hugely popular cafes which often adjoined the libraries. Florence personally chose the decor of each one, selecting the china, the furnishings and the style of lighting.

Elegant, smart and stocked with an enticing selection of drinks and light bites, the cafes attracted fashionable women with money and time on their hands. As Florence had envisaged, an outing to Boots became something of a social occasion, which generally included a change of reading material.

Libraries were often reached via a wide and imposing staircase, which led into a charming and welcoming area. Eric Spencer worked in the photographic department of Boots in Hammersmith and he recalls being intrigued by the behaviour of the store's very strict library manager. "He lined the staff up every morning," Eric remembers. "To check their appearance and issue orders. He was obsessed with the mahogany handrails on the staircase leading into the library. He made the staff polish them every day until they gleamed."

Lifts were provided when necessary and always courteously manned by an attendant. A ride in the lift was an exciting experience for young children in the early 20th century.

Boots' lifts would not have been as magnificent as the bronze Art Deco lifts installed at Selfridges in 1928 and staffed by glamorous female operators. These were badly damaged in the London Blitz and were not repaired until the war was over. The interior of a Selfridge's bronze lift can now be seen in the Museum of London's 20th Century Gallery.

Although cafes and libraries were seen as loss leaders they proved invaluable in raising the image of Boots shops and, in the longer term, they attracted a more affluent class of shopper.

The open shelving was an attractive feature, enabling borrowers to select their own books and the lower shelves were angled upwards, for easy viewing. The public libraries had only closed access. This meant customers had to search through the catalogue and remove the card relating to their chosen title, before presenting it to a member of staff, who would retrieve the book. Even if many subscribers preferred to be waited on by helpful staff, Boots could pride themselves on offering readers the opportunity to browse happily.

People could borrow books by leaving a deposit of half a crown (2s 6d) and then paying 1d or 2d per book. This provided an option for anyone unwilling, or unable, to part with a substantial sum of money at a given time.

Reduced subscriptions were available to trade unions, or specific occupational groups. There was also a postal service, especially for the housebound and people living in rural areas. Staff would wrap books up in brown paper, tie them with string but leave the ends open, enabling them to be charged at paper rate, rather than parcel rate. This was known as "Book Post" or "Printed Papers".

A tradition in Royal Mail decreed that printed matter should be sent at a cheaper rate than regular correspondence. Newspapers were dispatched free of charge before 1840. Parcels were left unsealed so that they could be checked for security reasons and also to ensure that regular letters had not been smuggled with the books.

The 1958 Post Office Guide states: *"Every printed paper is subject to examination in the post, and must, therefore, be posted without a cover, or in an unfastened cover, or in a cover which can be easily removed for the purpose of examination without breaking any seal or tearing any paper or separating any adhering surfaces or cutting any string. A packet posted without a cover may not be so fastened or otherwise treated as to prevent easy examination."*

In 1958, the book post rate was 2d for 2oz and under and 4d for 4oz and under. The maximum weight was 2lb.

Florence must have been delighted with the success of her libraries. With her attention to detail and enthusiasm for every aspect of the Boots business, she would almost certainly have taken an interest in titles bought for stock. One book Florence would have wanted to see on the shelves was "The Days I Knew" - Lillie Langtry's autobiography published in 1925.

Born on Florence's beloved Jersey in 1853, Lillie moved to London after marrying a wealthy widower. Due to her charm and good looks, she was soon the darling of society hostesses and also took to the stage, starring in many plays including "She Stoops to Conquer" performed in 1881 at London's Haymarket theatre. Known as the Jersey Lily, the actress's heyday as a society beauty culminated in her becoming a semi official mistress to the Prince of Wales, the future King Edward V11. Her lifestyle attracted huge media interest.

In her entertaining autobiography, Lillie recounts the story of her life with energy and humour. But she draws a discreet veil over her love affairs and refers to the Prince of Wales only as a friend. Boots subscribers may have been a little disappointed at the lack of scandalous revelations in Lillie's book but hundreds of them will have wanted to read it.

Florence would doubtless have been pleased when the famous actress was returned to the Channel Islands after her death in 1929. Lillie's final wish was to be buried in her parents' tomb at St. Saviour's Church in Jersey.

3. THE LIBRARY STAFF - A CUT ABOVE THE REST

"The whole secret of the successful librarian is the PERSONAL TOUCH. I believe that one of the most humanising experiences is the realisation that one has been of assistance to one's fellow man. There must, therefore, be a wealth of real happiness in the knowledge that one can so much influence the life of an individual to his or her profit and pleasure and to do it as part of one's daily livelihood."

Mr F. Richardson. Boots' Head Librarian. 1911-1941

Working in Boots Booklovers Library enhanced a girl's chances of making a good marriage, or so it was believed, in the heyday of the 1930s and 40's. It certainly helped improve social standing and provided opportunities for young staff to meet professional men, in a safe environment. Pat Oldale, who worked in several Bournemouth branches, recalls her manageress telling her that Library assistants were referred to as "Boot's young ladies". They certainly seem to have been encouraged to think of themselves as a cut above ordinary sales staff, although their rates of pay were no higher.

Opulent surroundings, with flower arrangements and mahogany shelves, transmitted a genteel allure even to relatively humble junior staff, who were nevertheless expected to replenish the flower vases from their own gardens and to apply elbow grease to the shelves.

Dorothy Rawlinson was fourteen years old when she began work at the Cleveleys branch of Boots in 1944. Her headmistress had recommended Dorothy for the position because she was the school librarian in her final year. It was company policy to recruit suitable girls in this way. Dorothy vividly remembers her manageress.

"Her name was Laura Isobel Terry. She was very strict and most precise in manner. I was so scared of her!"

For several weeks, Miss Terry didn't allow her youngest member of staff to do anything more complicated than dust the shelves and make sure all the books were in alphabetical order.

"I worked from 9am until 6pm Mondays to Saturdays, with Sundays off and a half day every Wednesday," Dorothy says. "I had to wear an overall, which I didn't mind because I thought it made me look business-like. I loved the job and still remember it with affection."

Dorothy is amongst many former members of staff who were kept firmly in line by the formidable women who ruled over their own little library empires. Boots Head Librarian was always a man but every branch was staffed exclusively by a team of young women, each supervised by a manageress - invariably a middle aged spinster.

Carol Worral worked at Boots in Leicester, with seven other members of staff.

"The manageress ruled us all with a rod of iron." Carol shudders. "She was very meticulous about everything. On Monday mornings, I had to remove the dust covers from all the books, then shake and fold each one." The dust covers were then put away until Saturday afternoon, when it was Carol's responsibility to replace them, to keep the books clean over the weekend. "It sounds simple," she says, with a wry smile. "But I remember being severely reprimanded once, for not doing the job properly."

Mavis Archer worked for Boots library in Nottingham, from 1952 - 1962. It was a happy time and she thought girls tended to stay because they enjoyed the work. But she too recalls a strict librarian.

"You had to mind your ps and qs," Mavis says. "I was ticked off once for *loitering*, when I stopped work for a couple of minutes to speak to a friend."

Joy Forrester-Addie was a reluctant Boots recruit. On leaving school in 1958 aged 16, Joy applied for a job in Bournemouth Borough Libraries but was told there were no current vacancies. At the time, Joy's mother worked for two retired teachers. These ladies were very old fashioned and most particular about the minutiae of their lives.

"They were kind hearted but snobbish," Joy says. "I suppose it was quite a feather in my cap when they offered to recommend me for a job at Boots library in Winton."

The former teachers were avid readers and class A borrowers. "Apparently they thought I was *the right sort of young lady* to serve subscribers." Joy grins. "I'm not quite sure why!"

Joy was very nervous at her interview with Mrs Lloyd - yet another formidable library manageress - and only began to feel more confident when asked about books she had read. "It was impressed on me that Boots library gave exceptional service to customers," she remembers. "It was clear that staff were expected to be unfailingly helpful and polite."

Joy encountered many class A subscribers who required special treatment. "I'm a **First** class reader, my dear." The general attitude was that public libraries were not for *people like them.*

"All the books had eyelet holes at the top of the spines, into which you put a tag when the book was borrowed," Joy says. "The class A subscribers had green tags and class B red ones. I can still picture them now, after all these years." Joy recalls a female customer who was a GP and who would only borrow books from the children's library, to be certain of avoiding any sexually explicit content.

Occasionally, books arrived at the Winton branch a short while before their publication date and had to be kept under wraps for a few days. "Some readers were desperate to lay their hands on popular titles," Joy says. "I remember a woman sneaking into our little office just to get a peep at "Bond Street Story", the latest book by Norman Collins."

There were three full time staff working at Winton and Joy remembers the library being always busy. The building was on three floors: the chemist at ground level, the library on the second floor and the staff room at the top. The stairs were narrow and rather rickety. "We always knew when customers were on their way," Joy says. "They made such a noise, clattering up those stairs."

Although Joy has fond memories of her year working for Boots, when she was offered a job in the public library, she accepted with alacrity.

It was Boots policy to employ school leavers and retain them until they married. The expectation was that girls would leave work soon after becoming engaged, ostensibly to give them time to prepare for married life. There was a marriage bar in many big companies and organisations but a desperate need for women workers during World War Two made it difficult to sustain.

The Post Office was a more enlightened employer than Boots, in this respect. Just before Christmas 1940, the Post Office called for women to volunteer as postwomen. Postmen were asked to bring along their *wives, sweethearts, sisters and lady friends* to help with seasonal mail delivery. Within hours of the announcement in London, 4,000 of the 8,000 women required had volunteered. In the Post Office, the marriage bar was abolished in 1946.

Boots employed widows during the Second World War but the company didn't abandon the marriage bar until the mid 1950s.

To counterbalance this rapid turnover of the workforce, spinster librarians remained in post until retirement, when they would be replaced by another of their ilk. Although many of these women were difficult and hard to work with, others are remembered with affection by former staff, some of whom even admired their elegance and dress sense. Jill Bennett worked in a busy Leicester branch and remembers that the librarian there had attended private school and was very well educated.

Miss Hannah-Marie Bednall began work at Boots library in Derby when she was fourteen, towards the end of the First World War. Her parents paid the considerable sum of £18, for their daughter to be accepted as an indentured apprentice.

This recruitment tool was one much favoured by the company over many years. In 2004, David Stathers retired from a senior management position with Boots after 44 years service. Albeit four decades after Hannah-Marie first took up her post in Derby library, he too began his working life with Boots as an indentured apprentice. The modern company continues to offer apprenticeship schemes.

Miss Bednall loved her job and is believed never to have missed a working day. Freddie Richardson - the man who spent thirty years giving every ounce of his devotion and energy to Boots - would have been delighted with her.

"The whole secret of the successful librarian is the PERSONAL TOUCH," declared Mr Richardson. *"I believe that one of the most humanising experiences is the realisation that one has been of assistance to one's fellow man. There must, therefore, be a wealth of real happiness in the knowledge that one can so much influence the life of an individual to his or her profit and pleasure and to do it as part of one's daily livelihood. Personal service to the reader on the one side, implicit obedience to the system on the*

*other - these things are the aim which will ultimately keep
the library department ever progressing."*

1924 was the year when Harold Abrahams and Eric Liddell
won gold medals at the Paris Olympics and the Sunday
Express became the first British newspaper to publish a
crossword. And on 23rd April 1924 - St George's Day - King
George V and Queen Mary opened the British Empire
Exhibition. It attracted 20 million visitors, which included
5000 Boots staff. On a sunny June day in 1924, they filled
eight trains, each carriage headed up as "Boots Wembley
Special". Theirs was by far the biggest single party to visit
the exhibition.

Elsie Matthews worked as a library assistant at Boots in
Middlesborough and also in Stockton on Tees.

"There was a staff outing to the Festival of Britain in 1951,"
remembers Elsie. "We were all very excited, especially as
the trip included tickets to look around the Royal Festival
Hall." This had cost £2 million to build and was officially
opened on 3rd May 1951, with a gala concert attended by
King George V1 and Queen Elizabeth, conducted by Sir
Malcolm Sargent and Sir Adrian Boult.

Elsie says staff welfare was important to the company. She
recalls an enduring and affectionate relationship between
the Boot family and their employees.

"I remember John Boot referring to the library girls as the
hostesses of his shops," she says. John was Jesse and
Florence's only son and like his parents, he was a generous
philanthropist.

After John had inherited his father's title and became 2nd Baron Trent, Nottingham University commissioned a portrait to be painted and hung in the university. "There was a sliding donation scheme to help pay for it," Elsie says. "The amount you were asked to give depended on your salary. I was more than happy to contribute my one shilling."

The portrait was presented to Nottingham University by the staff of Boots in March 1950. It was painted by Sir Oswald Hornby Joseph Birley and currently hangs in the Council Dining Room, Trent Building. The artist was a favourite of the Royal Family and he painted portraits of King George V, Queen Mary and Queen Elizabeth the Queen Mother.

John Eric Greenwood (known as Jenny Greenwood) was a rugby union international, who represented England from 1912 to 1920. He was a leading figure in the Golden Age of Rugger at King's College, Cambridge and also captained his country.

John Greenwood began working for Boots in 1920 and soon became a personal friend of Jesse and Florence. When he married, eighteen months after joining the company, the staff presented him with a wedding present of a large canteen of solid silver cutlery.

One Boots library assistant who left to write her own books, was the novelist Elizabeth Taylor. After leaving school in 1930, she was a governess for a while, before working as a junior assistant at Boots library in High Wycombe, Buckinghamshire.

Aspiring writers are naturally attracted to a bookish environment and Penny Vincenzi's first job - aged sixteen -

was with Harrods subscription library. As a junior assistant, Penny was allocated readers whose names began with the letter S. "Sir Malcolm Sargent was a sweetheart," Penny said. "Very polite." But apparently he was the exception. "Most customers were absolutely horrible."

Library assistants in both Harrods and Boots had to wear overalls. Dorothy Rawlinson quite liked this, believing it made her look more business-like but Penny loathed her Harrods overall: "A horrible green, so unflattering. Like joke cleaning-ladies' overalls." There were twelve desks in Harrods, each with one senior and two junior members of staff. Subscribers expected - and received - five star service.

"Customers got any book they wanted straight away," Penny remembers. "They just rang up and ordered it and the book was delivered that afternoon, sometimes by horse-drawn van."

Sometimes, Boots recruited their staff in ways that would seem quite irregular now. Susan Pulsford had a holiday job at Scarborough library in 1954 and absolutely loved the work. After she'd returned to school, the manageress paid a personal visit to her home, to tell Susan that a member of staff was leaving and the job was hers, if she wanted it.

"My parents wouldn't allow it," Susan says. "They insisted I continue with my education. I was disappointed at the time but they were probably right because Boots library in Scarborough only lasted a few more years."

Susan remembers serving Bessie Braddock, a Liverpool MP who was in Scarborough for the Labour Party Conference of 1954. An ardent socialist and fiery campaigner, *Battling Bessie* is often credited with entering into an exchange of insults with Winston Churchill, although the truth of the altercation is uncertain.

BB. "Winston, you are drunk and what's more, you are disgustingly drunk."

WC. "Bessie, my dear, you are ugly and what's more, you are disgustingly ugly. But tomorrow I shall be sober and you will still be disgustingly ugly."

Pat Oldale recalls serving Courtney Jones, a world champion ice skater in the 1950s and 60s. "He lived with his mother," Pat says, "and he often came in to choose books for her."

The singer and entertainer Anita Harris also remembers an encounter with the famous skater. As a little girl, Anita was often to be found at the Bournemouth ice rink on Westover Road, where she danced with Courtney Jones. "He was working for Hardy Amies as a dress designer by day and helping out the ice skaters by night."

Maureen Harris met famous actors while working at her branch of Boots in Bournemouth, where there were several theatres, such as the Winter Gardens and the Pavilion, as well as many smaller venues that no longer exist.

"Cary Grant came into the library when he was in Bournemouth visiting his mother," Maureen remembers. "Stewart Grainger was another regular. He owned a house on the East Cliff." Of course, no respectful Boots library assistant in the 1950s would have dreamed of requesting an autograph.

"I think I was lucky to work at a seaside branch because the clientele was more varied," Maureen says. During the winter months in Bournemouth, stars of stage and screen were replaced by wealthy visitors, who came to live in the town's most expensive hotels, before returning to the continent when the better weather arrived. Some of these temporary subscribers were very demanding and expected to be treated like royalty.

"There were a lot of retired military men of high rank. Admirals, Generals, Majors, Brigadiers - they all found their way to Boots library," Maureen says. "And their wives were used to being treated with great respect. I well remember one woman saying: *"My husband and I will be going to join Lady Docker on the yacht in the spring and I would like to have our books sent weekly to Cannes."*

Norah Docker was an English socialite who married three times, always choosing rich husbands. She loved notoriety and her third marriage to Sir Bernard Docker in 1949 was well documented for the couple's extravagant lifestyle.

The Dockers enjoyed visiting the French Riviera, until an incident in which Norah tore up a paper Monacan flag, which resulted in Prince Rainier banning her from Monaco. They had already been barred from the Monte Carlo Casino, after Norah slapped a waiter's face. The ban was soon extended to include the entire French Riviera.

Although few Boots subscribers were wealthy enough to associate with Lady Docker, many are remembered by former staff for a variety of reasons, generally because of their eccentric behaviour.

Ann Faragher, who worked in Berwick, isn't likely to forget the man who used to hurl his chosen book vaguely in the direction of the counter. "He never apologised if he scored a bulls-eye and hit one of the staff," Ann says. She also has vivid memories of a subscriber who brought his Irish wolfhound into the library. "The massive great dog would lower its head onto the counter and glower at me, as I discharged his master's book."

Maureen Harris remembers a truly terrifying customer named the Honourable Mrs Ferguson. This feisty lady was a retired School Inspectress, who must have struck fear into the hearts of many a head teacher when she arrived on the doorstep. Mrs Ferguson was of course a Class A subscriber and as an inexperienced junior assistant, Maureen was not permitted to serve such a lofty personage. But one day, on spotting this scary lady at the door, all the other staff scarpered and she was left to cope.

"My legs were shaking when I told Mrs Ferguson that I was on duty alone but would be very happy to help her if I could," Maureen says. "She wasn't too pleased at first but I found the books she'd ordered and she went off happily enough."

This turned out to be the start of quite a rapport between the cheerful young library assistant and the irascible old lady. On every visit, Mrs Ferguson would insist on being served by *her little girl*. "I rather enjoyed it," Maureen claims. "My colleagues thought I was mad but at least it got them off the hook!"

A few years later, when Mrs Ferguson had to endure the indignity of using the Lansdowne public library and being treated no differently from any ordinary person, she could still be heard querulously demanding to know how *her little girl* was getting on.

Branches were numbered and this was a generally accepted method used by staff to identify themselves, particularly on the telephone. Rather like army service numbers, these seem to be indelibly fixed in staff memories for evermore. Maureen remembers that her branch in Old Christchurch Road, Bournemouth was number 930 and Pat Oldale, a few miles further away, worked in branch number 932.

Each branch library had two counters. One was designated solely for Class A subscribers, who paid top rates and the other for Class B. New staff weren't allowed anywhere near the elite readers, until they had received thorough training on customer service. Affluence bought Class A subscribers respectful and personal service and they were never expected to choose their own books. A member of staff would bring a selection of titles to be perused and many might be discarded, before one was deemed acceptable. No subscriber ever left Boots library dissatisfied or empty handed.

However, mistakes will happen, despite the best of intentions. Carol Worral remembers a customer asking for a book for her son, who played for the Leicester Tigers and who was recovering from an injury. "I suggested "No Time for Fear" by Grantly Dick-Read, which I thought was a travel book," Carol explains. "But it turned out to be about the childbirth practices of African tribes!"

Grantly Dick-Read was a British obstetrician and the first president of the National Childbirth Trust. His book entitled "Childbirth Without Fear" was published in 1942 and became an international best-seller.

Staff were required to familiarise themselves with their readers' tastes and specific requests. Library lists were

compiled by Class A subscribers, who were allowed to make
their choice from any available books, with no restrictions.
The more humble Class B subscribers were left to search
the shelves themselves, choosing their own books and
forced to eye recent titles wistfully, knowing that those
desirable best sellers were out of reach, until they were a
year old. Books could be returned to any Boots branch.

Class A subscribers were actively encouraged to request
new books, which on arrival were put in the Bespoke Room,
until they were collected. There was a forbidden and
intriguing aura around this room and Class B subscribers in
particular were always curious to know what was secreted
away, out of view.

Elsie Matthews remembers four deliveries a week of new
and requested titles, at her Middlesbrough branch in the
1940s. These came by train and were brought to Boots by
the railway wagon. Unpacking the boxes of books was a
popular job.

One of the biggest best-sellers of all time was first
published in 1946 and must have taken pride of place in
many of Boots' Bespoke Rooms. Benjamin Spock's "Baby
and Child Care" was full of contentious ideas about
parenting, greatly at odds with "Feeding and Care of Baby"
by Frederic Truby King, considered the definitive guide to
the first year of life.

The Truby King method was to feed baby strictly by the
clock every four hours and preferably never at night. He
urged parents to put children to sleep in their own
bedrooms from day one and to stoically ignore pitiful wails
of hunger. Truby King recommended leaving babies in their

prams in the garden for hours on end - no matter how chilly the weather - to toughen them up.

He also advised restricting cuddles to ten minutes a day. In his view, parenting was primarily about routine, discipline and detachment. The formative months were for eating, sleeping and growing - not bonding.

By contrast, Dr Spock advocated a more empathetic approach to bringing up children and told parents to have confidence in their own instincts and common sense. His message to mothers was: "*Trust yourself. You know more than you think you do.*" Spock's guide to parenting encouraged affection and spontaneity, warmth and love. It urged couples to see their children as unique individuals, all of whom would respond to situations differently.

Ann Faragher says the staff knew which ladies enjoyed a spicy read but were too embarrassed to admit it. In 1956 the novel "Peyton Place" by Grace Metalious would definitely have fitted this category. First published in America, it sold 60,000 copies in the first ten days after its release. Incest, abortion, adultery, lust and murder are recurring themes in this story of a small community hiding sordid secrets. The book was banned in Ireland in 1958, for being obscene and indecent.

Apparently many subscribers expected their favourite authors to write books practically on a monthly basis. Barbara Cartland was a woman who did her best to rise to the challenge, becoming one of the most prolific and commercially successful authors of the 20th century. Between 1925 and her death in 2000, she wrote 723 books, eighteen of which were published in 1975. When Barbara Cartland died, she left a total of 160 unpublished novels.

Girls starting work in the 1950s had slender wardrobes. Rationing didn't finally end until 1953 and serviceable clothes were only discarded when they became shabby or threadbare. Maureen Harris remembers wearing her school uniform to work underneath her overall and fifteen year old Pat Oldale went bare legged to her interview because she didn't own a pair of stockings.

"After offering me the job, I was told I must wear stockings at work," Pat says. "As though I wouldn't have worn them to my interview, if I possessed any! I think I had to borrow my sister's, until I was paid."

Subscribers were often very generous at Christmas time, giving presents of chocolates and biscuits. Jill Bennett remembers an old gentleman at her library in Leicester, who liked to hide his seasonal gift of chocolates somewhere amongst the shelves, for a member of staff to stumble across.

Jill also recalls an elderly female subscriber, who gave the library manageress a sealed envelope just before Christmas. "We thought there had to be at least one pound note inside," Jill says. "And we were all told to make a point of thanking the woman for our present. So it was a bit of a let-down when the envelope turned out to be empty!"

The occasional subscriber proved memorable for quite extraordinary reasons. Maureen Harris has vivid memories of the Incident Of The Dog In The Basket. An elderly lady regularly visited the library, carrying a wicker basket covered with a cushion, on top of which lay a small dog. One day, she was spotted secreting a book underneath the cushion, before heading for the counter and having another book checked out in the usual way.

"For three months I played detective," Maureen remembers. "I shadowed the woman, watching her behave in exactly the same way each time. She always put the illicitly borrowed book back on the shelf - usually in the wrong place - so no actual theft took place."

With the evidence stacked up against her, the culprit was finally confronted by the manageress, as she left the library one day with her usual two books, one lawfully borrowed and the other hidden beneath the cushion on which her little dog dozed.

The old lady was distraught when she was told that because of her misdemeanours, her subscription was being revoked. Eventually the Boots bosses relented and it was agreed that if she left her dog at home and came into the library carrying only one small bag, she would be allowed to resume borrowing books. But like everyone else, only one at a time.

"I was pleased they found a compromise," Maureen says. "Because that old lady loved reading and loved her books. It would have been cruel to ban her from the library."

Due to the marriage bar and consequent high turnover of staff, plus illness and holidays, the library system depended very much upon the relief worker. Once a member of staff reached the age of twenty-one, she could be called upon to help out at any branch. This was a prospect which excited some girls and terrified others. Staff on the Channel Islands and the Isle of Man could be sent to mainland Britain, sometimes for an unspecified length of time.

The arrangement ensured that before a member of staff reached the top of the career ladder, she had gained invaluable experience of work in a variety of libraries, some situated in a busy city, a few in rural communities and others in seaside resorts. This enabled her to make mature and sensible decisions, based on the cumulative knowledge of these branches and their subscribers.

When Boots removed the marriage bar in the mid 1950s, married women were not exempt from doing relief work, which made it difficult for those with family commitments.

Although every Boots library had subtle and specific differences, generally speaking the corporate image prevailed and there were no fundamental disparities in regime or atmosphere. Pat Oldale recalls the importance attached to the Revised Instructional Circular Letters, a copy of which was held at every branch. These RICLs held the answer to any and every situation that might arise.

After their initial training, new staff were required to take examinations, one of which tested their understanding of the Boots circulating system, as detailed in the RICLs. Other papers tested book knowledge, to enable library assistants to meet the requirements of their subscribers. They were issued with examination guidance notes and time off was given to study and revise. The papers covered every genre, including detective stories, light romance, family stories, biographies, current affairs, books about sport, the sea, the country and many more.

These examinations were specific to Boots and were therefore not recognised by the public libraries or any professional bodies. But when staff sought work elsewhere, after Boots Booklovers Library closed in the 1960s, they believed their qualifications were given genuine respect by prospective employers and in particular, the public libraries.

Many former staff comment on the excellence of the training they received. Jill Bennett went to London on a training course in the late 1950s and remembers visiting the buying offices and the library warehouse, known as W12. "The company put us up in a hotel for the week," Jill remembers. "We were all very young and it was tremendously exciting."

Jill won an uncorrected proof copy of a book, as a prize for gaining top marks in one of the exams. Uncorrected proof copies contain errors that are rectified at the final stage of production. On very rare occasions, such books can be extremely valuable. In July 2013, an uncorrected UK proof of "Midnight's Children" by Salman Rushdie, sold for £8,454.

Jill's award would seem to have been unusual. Prizes given to library assistants who took part in competitions or who were nominated for good service, were generally handsomely bound copies of great works of fiction.

Mavis Archer also sat the exams and was sent on a couple of training courses in London.

"I well remember being shown around the Oxford University Press and staying in a Temperance hotel," she says. The Temperance Movement, promoting moderation in the consumption of alcohol - or better still total abstention - started in Britain in the 1830s and became very prominent in Victorian times. In the first half of the 20th century, there were Temperance inns and hotels in every British town and city.

The Cross Keys Temperance Inn at Cautley in Cumbria, is now the only remaining English pub without a liquor license. In 1902, the landlord died trying to save an intoxicated visitor who had fallen into the River Rawthey. The inebriated man survived and his family bought the Inn, stipulating in its deeds that it could never sell alcohol again. However, visitors are allowed to bring along their own bottles and corkscrews are provided.

Maureen Harris went on a week long training course in London in the late 1950s and recalls a visit to W12 HQ, to learn how the order system worked and the way in which books were distributed throughout the country. "We were given tickets to see "West Side Story" one evening," Maureen says. "It was so exciting. We all had a wonderful time."

Leonard Bernstein's "West Side Story" opened at Her Majesty's Theatre on the Haymarket in December 1958 and starred George Chakiris as Riff. The musical enjoyed a run of 1,039 performances, until its final show in 1961.

Pat Oldale remembers her training course in London and the thrill of staying at the Ivanhoe - a Temperance hotel - and going to see "The Flower Drum Song" at the Palace Theatre.

There seems no doubt that former staff remember their years spent in Boots libraries with great nostalgic affection and many might agree with Maureen when she says - "I still think we had the better times, when the customers came first and work was to be enjoyed and not just tolerated."

4. FLORENCE AND HER "DEAR GIRLS"

"It is one of my greatest joys in life that I am able to stretch out a helping hand to so many young girls. I would like you all to know that in any time of serious difficulty or trouble, I will always be your sincere friend."

Florence Boot. 1906

Florence was a remarkable female figure in the male dominated world of business in the Victorian era. She was a good-looking woman of striking appearance, always elegantly dressed, gregarious and with a forceful personality.

Florence did not allow the birth of her first child to limit her commitment to the company or to the growth of its embryo libraries. Born in 1889, John Boot was taken to work in his carrycot at an early age and his mother fed him in her office. No one would have dared to challenge Florence, although such behaviour was practically unheard of amongst respectable, well-to-do women. Following the death of a second son in infancy, Florence and Jesse had two daughters, Dorothy and Marjorie.

Florence possessed a lively social conscience. She was a pioneer of staff welfare, taking a personal interest in female employees, whether they worked in Boots shops, libraries, factories or warehouses. She regarded it as her duty to ensure the physical and moral wellbeing of the girls and young women employed by the company. But it wasn't just duty which motivated Florence. She was generous and kind, referring to the female staff as her "Dear Girls" and taking a motherly interest in their lives and families.

Florence's particular concern for working class girls was rooted in her own memories of serving in her father's shop in Jersey.

"My earliest recollections are of toddling around the counters at my father's side and learning from him that all labour was dignified and that to be courteous and obliging was a great asset in the business world and that life in a shop could and ought to be a high calling."

When Boots stores and libraries expanded into dozens of British high streets, Florence would travel any distance to help resolve a problem faced by one of her Girls in the branches. Women who were off work due to illness or family bereavement were quite likely to find the boss's wife standing on their doorstep, offering a warm embrace and a thoughtful gift.

On hearing that some young women arrived at work without having had any breakfast, Florence arranged for them to be given a mug of hot cocoa first thing every morning. Each Christmas she sent all her Girls a silk banner, printed with a moral verse, for encouragement and in appreciation of their work during the year.

In 1913, this read:

"Better a smile than a tear or a sigh,

Better a laugh than a Frown.

Better an Upward Look to the Sky,

Than always a sad look down.

The Joys we find in each Little Day

Perhaps may seem Few and Small,

But better these little Joys, I say,

Than to have no Joys at all.

Keep Faith in the Love that Blesses men,

As the Sunshine does the Sad.

Let us do our Best and Trust the Rest

To the Loving Heart of God."

In 1911, Florence recruited a trained welfare worker named Eleanor Kelly, as her assistant. Eleanor suggested several improvements, included a surgery at one of the Nottingham stores, which employed nurses and a part time doctor. Home visiting schemes were introduced and financial assistance for female employees in straitened circumstances. Eleanor also helped women access help from the Salvation Army and local churches. By the 1920s, Boots had a flourishing welfare department, whose staff managed the surgery and first aid rooms.

Florence was an enthusiastic advocate of further education. She spearheaded the provision of classes leading to useful qualifications for all members of staff and everyone was strongly encouraged to attend them. There were no fees to pay and tea was provided beforehand, so they would be in the best frame of mind to study and with no reason to arrive late for lessons. In less than a year, nearly 600 young people had attended the classes.

But Florence well understood that the domestic circumstances of many women would make it impossible for them to take advantage of such opportunities for further education. In 1913, she wrote to the female staff, offering reassurance: *"My Dear Girls. Lest any of you should think that because I have taken up the cause of the College girl, you may be in any danger of losing your position or salary, I want to assure you that such will not be the case. Your salaries will be raised rather than lowered. I want to help **all** girls, to whatever class they belong, to help each other and to help themselves."*

Because Florence was friendly and extrovert herself, she recognised the value of social interaction, which led her to arrange regular staff trips and excursions. The first recorded event was a modest picnic in 1888 but this small beginning was followed by more adventurous outings, to local beauty spots or the seaside. Staff were transported in charabancs to Hazelford Ferry beside the River Trent, or to the fields at Plumtree. A hearty picnic was always provided, followed by a leisurely stroll or team games for the youngsters.

In 1894, Boots commissioned a special train to take staff to the Castleton Caverns in Derbyshire and the company celebrated this event with a souvenir brochure. 1894 saw the opening of the Hope Valley railway line, so hundreds of people would have flocked to Castleton that year. Clearly, Florence wanted her Girls to experience the excitement of being amongst the first visitors to the caverns.

In 1902, Florence took 500 lady clerks and Nottingham warehouse staff to Skegness. They arrived mid morning and made straight for the beach, where paddling in the chilly North sea waves was top of everyone's wish list. At midday it was off to the Pavilion, for a slap-up meal of roast beef, apple pie and jellies and cream. The afternoon was spent watching the antics of a band of Pierrots.

Pierrot shows, with their distinctive black and white clown costumes, pointy hats and pom-poms were hugely popular in British seaside resorts from the 1890s to the 1950s. The style of entertainment encouraged a close bond between the performer and the audience, using jokes, sketches and comic songs about everyday life. Gracie Fields' career as a singer and comedienne began in a Pierrot troupe. In 1914, she earned £3 a week, performing at St Anne's-on-Sea, with" Cousin Freddy's Pierrot Concert Party".

In 1908, to mark Florence's forty fifth birthday, almost one hundred female staff were taken by train to visit the Franco-British exhibition at Wembley. In appreciation of her generosity and as an expression of their affection, Florence's Girls presented her with a large decorated book, signed by every member of the outing.

The Franco-British Exhibition was a huge public fair held in London to commemorate the signing of the Entente Cordiale in 1904. British royalty flocked there, rubbing shoulders with President Fallieres of France and a Russian

Grand Duchess. Twenty elaborate white palaces were built and 120 exhibition centres erected, plus a scenic railway and an entire Irish village, named Ballymaclinton.

Before every expedition, Florence wrote personally to parents of the youngest female staff, assuring them that chaperons would be in attendance to guarantee the safety of their daughters. She believed it was both a duty and a privilege to look after the physical and moral wellbeing of the many girls and women employed by the company.

In a letter dated 1906, Florence says: *"It is one of my greatest joys in life that I am able to stretch out a helping hand to so many young girls. I would like you all to know that in any time of serious difficulty or trouble, I will always be your sincere friend."*

As a girl growing up in St Helier, Florence was a Sunday School teacher and an active member of the Methodist chapel where she and Jesse met. Her faith continued to be an integral part of her life and she organised regular meetings for Boots' female employees, with talks from visiting clergymen. When girls left the company to be married, Florence gave them a Bible as a leaving present.

Jesse built a new home for his growing family near Trent Bridge. He named it Plaisaunce and Florence decorated the house with all her usual energy and creative skill. There was a dance hall and elegant tearooms, as well as many acres of parkland which were used for tennis matches and athletic events, specifically for the teams of Boots employees who were beginning to participate in sports contests nationally.

Florence used her beautiful new home to treat her Girls to tea parties and musical concerts on summer Sunday afternoons. These would finish with hymn singing, after which the young women were taken home in a fleet of horse drawn buggies. Many library staff will have been amongst the employees who enjoyed these treats and outings.

Jesse bought a large house in Nottingham, which his wife named St Helier, in affectionate memory of the town in which she had been raised and where she met her husband. The exuberant Florence lost no time decorating their new home with her usual combination of style, warmth and elegance and filling it with guests.

By nature a reserved man and in constant pain from worsening arthritis, Jesse did not wholeheartedly share this enthusiasm for entertaining. Nevertheless, he hosted dinners and social gatherings which included many famous visitors, such as the Liberal Prime Minister, Lord Asquith. Jesse was a loyal supporter of the Liberal Party and in recognition of this and also his many philanthropic works, he was knighted in 1909.

Amidst all this excitement, Lord and Lady Boot did not forget their retired staff, some of whom were experiencing hardship. The Dorothy Boot Homes, in Wilford near Nottingham, were named after their eldest daughter. Built in 1908, they were intended to supply accommodation to former employees who were veterans of the Crimean War (1854-1856) and the Indian Mutiny (1857-1858).

The Dorothy Boot Homes comprised eleven houses, all provided rent-free and each with its own bath and a garden. Residents were supplied with medical care and had access to a clubroom, which was equipped with newspapers and a library. They were treated to a monthly social party and allowed to accept respectable employment to supplement their income. As each veteran passed away, his house was offered for *"the use and enjoyment of aged and deserving persons."*

Boots also purchased properties with a view to using them as convalescent and holiday homes. In 1912, Jesse announced that staff who made weekly contributions to the Hospital Fund would be entitled to two or three weeks stay at these establishments.

While the majority were available to both men and women, Florence ensured that a few houses were allocated specifically to her Girls. A Leicestershire convalescent home acquired by Boots in 1912 was solely for girls and women and was co-administered by the Nottingham Sunday School Union.

Many special events, such as pageants, prize competitions and outings, were led by organisations such as the Nottingham Sunday School Union, which represented a variety of Christian churches within the city.

Rules observed by the children of Castle Gate Sunday School, Nottingham in 1836:

1) The *Children are expected to pay attention to the instructions of their Teachers and to behave towards them with affection and respect. If any play truant, be guilty of gross misbehaviour, or be disorderly in their conduct during Divine Worship, they shall in the first instance be reproved and afterwards, if the case require, be punished.*

2) Rewards will be occasionally distributed amongst those Children who distinguish themselves by their attendance, good behaviour and improvement.

The Boots Girls' Holiday Home opened in 1920 at Trusthorpe, on the Lincolnshire coast. Named "The Laurels", it was hired for the summer months and was for the particular benefit of Nottingham female staff aged eighteen to twenty four. Those who visited were called "Trussyites". The holidays came rent-free and the girls only paid for any additional expenses they accrued.

The Laurels had a resident matron, who took charge of her visitors welfare.   Boots staff magazine "The Beacon" commended the home, describing it as: *"An ideal house, in a splendid situation for a real, fresh air, seaside holiday and Mrs Daft, who will mother the home, will soon be a friend to all."*

The health benefits of a change of scene, coupled with fun, friendship and relaxation, was soon apparent and in 1922, a surplus of £10,000 from the Boots Insurance Society enabled more homes to be purchased.

"Windyhaugh", on the promenade at Skegness, was opened in 1922 and was used by staff as a convalescent and holiday home. Another house named "The Retreat" at Barton in Nottinghamshire, provided accommodation for a maximum of six young women, who were encouraged to take long, healthy walks in the countryside.

The strain of working even longer hours during the First World War, had taken a cruel toll on Jesse's health. Almost seventy years old and with painful arthritis, Jesse was spending nearly every day in a wheelchair, unable to give the company the attention it deserved. His arthritis was so bad that anyone wishing to shake his hand had to be careful to apply only the very lightest pressure.

There was mounting discontent amongst Boots' managers and a growing pile of letters asking for increases in salary, to which the only reply they received was that their boss was too ill to deal with the matter. Jesse was frugal all his life and very different from Florence, who enjoyed spending money and was by nature generous and extravagant.

Jesse had no confidence in his son or any of the senior employees and he had decided that his family should not inherit the business when he died. So Jesse began to look around for a likely buyer and his attention settled on the United Drug Company, one of the largest pharmaceutical firms in America. He invited Louis Liggett - its CEO - to visit him in Nottingham but Florence, who was very much opposed to selling the company, managed to stave off a meeting between the two men. But despite the storm of protest from his family, Jesse was determined to put his business up for sale.

Eventually Liggett made an offer of £2¼ million, a phenomenal sum of money in 1920. Although Jesse did not care for Liggett - a loud, strident extrovert - he immediately accepted the American's offer. The press promptly besieged the family home, much to Florence's indignation. One reporter found his way into the house but regretted his audacity when Lady Boot beat him over the head with a rolled up newspaper, shouting: *"Get out, you beast!"*

Staff were very upset by the American takeover and many older workers feared they would lose their jobs. John Boot was devastated by his father's actions and regarded it as little consolation when Jesse made sure Liggett offered him a managerial position.

The father/son relationship had always been difficult. Jesse considered John to be little more than a rich playboy, who could certainly not be trusted to make business decisions. John loved the stage and enjoyed nothing more than a trip to London to see a play, returning home in the early hours, on the mail train. Unfortunately for him, his father was an early riser. Up at 6 am, it was Jesse's custom to have a massage to relieve his arthritis, before reading the newspapers and sitting down to breakfast. So it was with grim disapproval, that he sometimes witnessed his son's arrival home via the night mail train, after a night in town.

However, John's experiences during armed combat in the First World War had left him much chastened and with a far more mature attitude. There was no altering Jesse's mind about his son's character but Louis Liggett recognised the young man's untapped business potential and Boots' change of ownership signalled an unexpected upturn in John's fortunes.

Much to Jesse's surprise, his son took on a leading role in the company's development. Thirteen years later, with the support of a group of influential bankers, John succeeded in buying the company back from Louis Liggett and Boots was once again in British hands.

Despite deteriorating health, Jesse was reluctant to withdraw entirely into retirement and he donated a considerable amount of his vast fortune towards the building of a new University College in Nottingham. He couldn't resist becoming personally involved in every aspect of this project, even advising on suitable positioning for flower borders.

Florence also took an active interest in the development and she personally funded the building of a women's hall of residence. Named the Florence Boot Hall, it opened on 24th November 1928, with accommodation for one hundred female students. Florence insisted that the hall should be set up in an informal, homely way, conducive to a friendly and sociable atmosphere, which she herself enjoyed on the frequent occasions she dropped in for a cup of tea with the students.

In 1929, Jesse was elevated to the peerage, as Baron Trent of Nottingham. Meanwhile, John Boot was proving himself to be as hard working and as shrewd a businessman as his father and as committed a philanthropist, with continuing emphasis on staff welfare. Employee insurance and pension schemes were protected and there was a programme of regular social outings and sports events.

Florence must have been delighted when the company opened another holiday home at Great Missenden in Buckinghamshire, following the onset of WWII. "The Knowle" was intended primarily for female staff living in towns that had been severely blitzed and who badly needed a week's rest in comparative peace and safety. Boots paid all accommodation costs and deducted nothing from the women's salaries.

"The Knowle" housed twelve women and provided such facilities as a lounge, a piano, wireless and an assortment of indoor and outdoor games. By the end of the war, around 4,000 of the 11,000 female employees had visited the retreat. Selection was made by supervisors and the company's doctor. The matron at "The Knowle" was required to submit a progress report for each guest.

Towards the end of Jesse's life, he and Florence spent a lot of time at their Jersey home - Villa Millbrook - situated near the sea front at St Aubin's Bay. But Jesse also bought a house at Cannes, which he named Villa Springlands. Florence loved taking holidays in the South of France and she encouraged her husband to enjoy life as best he could, in spite of his crippling arthritis. She went to extraordinary lengths to ensure Jesse's comfort.

When they travelled to Cannes, Florence hired a special invalid carriage to be attached to the train from Calais, so that Jesse could remain in his own bed during the journey to the South of France. She also employed a doctor and a Swiss nurse to be in constant attendance when her husband was travelling.

Florence loved entertaining and enjoyed being spontaneous. She would often get into conversation with people during a morning shopping trip in Cannes and impulsively invite her newfound friends to lunch that same day. Fortunately, her chef was an accommodating fellow and he most probably adored his charming employer.

After Jesse died in 1931, thousands of Islanders lined the funeral route from St Helier Parish Church to the family vault in St Brelade.

After her husband's death, Florence had the old chapel at Millbrook completely refurbished in his memory. She also commissioned Rene Lalique - her neighbour in Cannes - to transform the local church of St Matthew. Lalique's glass installations include the font, altar rail, cross and pillars and the unique Glass Church has become one of Jersey's primary attractions.

On the occasion of George VI's coronation, Florence donated some land for public use, on condition that it should be used: *"for the young to play and the old to rest."*

When Florence was on holiday in Egypt with her grandchildren she met the Scottish nobleman and pioneering aviator Lord Clydesdale, who was chief pilot on the first flight over Mount Everest in 1933. He persuaded Florence to let him take her up in his airplane and she enjoyed the flight so much that afterwards she flew everywhere. There was no airport on Jersey, so when she flew back home the pilot had to land on the beach.

Florence was always beautifully dressed and most of her clothes were made in Paris. One wardrobe was devoted solely to fur coats. She had an impressive collection of silver and when the Germans occupied Jersey in 1940, her enterprising chef buried it in the chicken run. A wise precaution because the Germans took over Villa Millbrook for an officers' mess.

Florence managed to get away from Jersey before the invasion. A Scottish village provided sanctuary for much of the war and Florence often delighted her neighbours by holding one of her extravagant parties, inviting everyone in the village from the postmistress to the garage man. On her return to Jersey, the silver was dug up from its hiding place and doubtless the chef was generously rewarded for his initiative.

Even as an old lady, Florence never lost her zest for life or her gregarious nature. She enjoyed a daily drive around the

Island in her green, chauffeur driven Rolls Royce. Florence liked these excursions to be taken at a very low speed so she could see all that was happening around her. She always took a supply of gifts, which she would hand out, often to children. This largesse ranged from half a dozen eggs, to her trademark present of a bottle of perfume.

Florence continued to take a personal interest in her staff, many of whom had been with her for decades. Once a month, they all lined up and waited to be invited into her study, where she would be sitting at a desk, piled high with wads of bank notes. Besides paying their wages she liked to chat with each employee, hearing news about their families.

Florence died at her home in Jersey on 17th June 1952, aged eighty-nine. John Boot - now 2nd Baron Trent - outlived his mother by only four years, dying at the relatively early age of sixty-seven. He left Boots securely established as one of the largest companies in Britain, with international interests and a turnover of millions.

John's attitude to staff welfare reflected that of his parents: *"When we build factories in which it is a joy to work, when we establish pension funds which relieve our workers of fears for their old age, when we reduce the number of working days in the week, or give long holidays with pay to our retail assistants, we are setting a standard which Governments in due time will be able to make universal."*

5. THE IDEAS MAN - NOT ALL OF THEM POPULAR

"We must, above all things, pull together. There are, however, some librarians who cannot grip the imperial point of view. The application of our system must be absolutely uniform throughout and I want all librarians to hold to this idea closely. I have previously explained that I liken our library system to a bicycle wheel, the Head Librarian's office being represented by the hub, the Branches the spokes and the System the rim. Any faultiness in the spokes jeopardises the rim at the service point of contact. So it is with our System."

Freddie Richardson. 1922.

When Boots Library HQ moved to London in 1901, Mercer Stretch acquired an assistant, to help shoulder his rapidly growing workload. Mr W. J Roberts came from Torquay, where he had worked in the well-respected Iredale's bookshop, an establishment that also housed a private library.

Iredale's reading rooms proclaimed themselves to be: *"The Finest and Most Luxurious in the Provinces, with a Boudoir set apart for the use of Ladies and a Smoking Room for Gentlemen."*

Iredale's catered for wealthy seaside visitors, who wished to read the latest books whilst relaxing and enjoying the sea air. If required, staff would personally deliver books to customers' hotels in Torquay and the surrounding area.

So Mr Robert's credentials were impeccable and he would have been well able to deal with the expectations of Boots' middle class subscribers. A few years later, when Mercer Stretch moved to Harrods Library, Mr Roberts succeeded him as Head Librarian.

But the individual who brought most drive and enthusiasm to the top job was a man named Freddie Richardson. He worked for thirteen years in Mitchell's Royal Library, at 33 Old Bond Street London, which supplied books to Queen Victoria.

In 1905, Richardson left Mitchell's to become assistant manager at the newly opened Times Book Club. A year later, he joined Boots Booklovers Library as warehouse superintendent, where his ability was soon recognised and in 1911 he was offered the job of Head Librarian.

Richardson understood the importance of advertising and he used every channel possible to promote the library. He improved on previous catalogues, producing even more detailed ones, with introductions which emphasised the numerous benefits available to subscribers.

In 1919, the periodical list was headed up: "*Please glance at our Special Offers on the next page and page 3 of the cover, and having glanced, please ponder over them.*"

Prominence was given to the location of Boots libraries in most of the important towns and cities in the country, such as London, Manchester, Liverpool and Birmingham. Subscribers were promised superb library decor, with modern shelving and fittings. *"Our methods in this direction have been described as the **Last Word in Library Construction**."* Framed lists of additions to stock were displayed outside every store which had a library.

Richardson was keen to encourage the sale of second hand books and made a feature of special offers, to extend their popularity. Selling surplus stock became a fundamental way for Boots to recoup some of their expenditure and proved very popular with the general public. In 1913, a three volume set of the first edition of the ***Life and Letters of Queen Victoria*** was available second-hand for 6s 9d.

Advertisements for the library were placed at the back of all Pelham Library Books, which were published by Boots and sold in their book department. This series was named after the company's shop at Pelham Street, in Nottingham's fashionable town centre. With its many splendid features, including a gallery supported by a colonnade of cast iron pillars and mahogany counters, this became the model for future Boots stores.

Richardson wrote a series of articles for the company magazine "The Bee", in which he encouraged staff to do their utmost to make Boots Booklovers Library the most successful in the land. Their emblem was The Little Green Shield and this crest took pride of place in the window of each Boots store which had a library. Richardson took every opportunity to remind staff that they should be proud of this shield, which symbolised "*The Most Efficient and Accommodating Library Service in the Kingdom*".

In an article published in March 1923, Richardson wrote: "*I want to encourage every librarian to do her utmost for the remaining period of this year. The meaning of the Little Green Shield should be reflected at the branches in:*

1) Excellence of the Service.

2) Exhibition of courtesy on all and every occasion.

3) A thorough knowledge of, and a keen pleasure in, the work on the part of every librarian."

Richardson was keen to keep up the numbers of new subscribers and in December 1923 he urged staff to remember that: "*A Christmas gift of a library subscription is by way of being a novelty but it has nothing flimsy or useless about it. It is a real present and lasts a twelvemonth. If you have a chance of settling a doubt so often expressed as to what shall be given as a Christmas present, plump for a library subscription... but do not wait to hear the doubt expressed.*"

Boots diligent Head Librarian was equally keen to urge staff in seaside resorts not to let slip any opportunity to recruit new subscribers during the summer months.

"*Every librarian should see that a good stock of Short Date Prospectuses is on hand, not only in the library department but - with the co-operation of the branch manager - available on counters throughout the shop.*"

And furthermore: *"Many local papers, especially in the smaller resorts, advertise the names of visitors and frequently their temporary residence is also quoted. A Short Date Prospectus delivered to these persons would not be wasted."*

Freddie Richardson strove to make staff aware of the importance of the Prospectus at every opportunity and in 1927 he made the following suggestions:

"Try to distribute the Prospectus to all the residential districts in your neighbourhood. Make a practice of selecting the address of one of your subscribers, turning up the Road, Gardens or Avenue in the Directory and sending at least half a dozen Prospectuses to your subscribers' neighbours. Make a habit of doing this EACH DAY."

Every branch took pride in its attractive, modern appearance and the company liked to stress its reputation for providing the last word in library construction. Richardson recognised the value of a high quality, corporate image and was irritated by staff who were lax in their attitude to this. In September 1922, he used the pages of the "Bee" to hammer his message home.

*"We must, above all things, pull together. There are, however, some librarians who cannot grip the imperial point of view. The application of our system must be **absolutely uniform throughout** and I want all librarians to hold to this idea closely. I have previously explained that I liken our library system to a bicycle wheel, the Head Librarian's office being represented by the hub, the Branches the spokes and the System the rim. Any faultiness in the spokes jeopardises the rim at the service point of contact. So it is with our System."*

Richardson was prepared to make use of the carrot, as well as the stick. He introduced competitions between branches for the highest number of new subscribers, or the greatest number of renewals, achieved in a given timespan. In August 1927, a set of twelve volumes entitled "Masterpieces of Literature" was the enticing prize. These days - and perhaps even then - a bottle of fizz and a box of chocolates might prove more tempting.

But librarians did their share of promoting Boots products, as demonstrated several times in the STAR SALES column of the "Bee". The following extract in May 1923 must have brought a satisfied smile to Richardson's face.

"A subscriber at branch 1121 (Warrington) called into the library to pay her subscription and showed an interest in our Fancy Goods display. Miss M. Price took a keen interest and demonstrated a series of items to the lady, as result of which volume amount to £4/10/0 was made."

Miss Price was not the only librarian to be awarded a gold star. Miss E Barber, of branch 232 (Walsall) also used her initiative in February 1923.

"Miss Barber conceived the idea of suspending from a counter stand on the side table in the library, a series of Lavender Globes, and as result, in about the course of a month, £9/18/6 had been added to the takings and this without in any way interfering with Miss Barber's legitimate work."

Library detectives were one of Richardson's innovations. If a manager suspected there was a thief lurking behind the mahogany bookshelves, it was her duty to inform the Head Librarian, who would send a detective to investigate. Theft on a regular scale would seem to have been surprisingly prevalent amongst refined Booklovers, to warrant such a dedicated team of crime busters.

The culprit was often found to be a kleptomaniac old lady, who would be let off with a caution and her subscription cancelled. It took a long time to catch up with a light fingered clergyman, who was regularly making off with Boots' books, possibly hidden in the folds of his cassock. He managed to steal over 300 library books, before the illicit collection was discovered at his home.

Freddie Richardson kept his finger very firmly on the library pulse and made it his business to know exactly what was going on at each branch and at every level of operations. Nothing was too mundane for his attention. Every branch was required to keep daily count of:

1) Number of new subscriptions and which subscription bracket was applicable.

2) Number of books borrowed.

3) How many books were requested at each branch.

4) Sales of second hand copies.

Every day at noon, Richardson was presented with a hefty folder containing all this information. He then spent untold hours analysing the figures and comparing them with those of the previous day. Woe betide any branch whose tally regularly went in the wrong direction.

Freddie Richardson does not seem to have been a man overly concerned with his own popularity rating. He introduced a team of library inspectresses, who operated along very similar lines to those of the modern day mystery shopper. These women must surely have been viewed as snoopers by library managers and their interference both resented and feared.

They visited branches unannounced and sent written reports back to Richardson. Their task was to ensure that the rigorous standards laid down by the Head Librarian were strictly adhered to. Naturally, any criticism resulting from their visits tended to upset library staff. But this initiative almost certainly contributed to the efficiency and inexorable growth of Boots Booklovers Library in the 1920s and 1930s.

One of Richardson's main tasks was the selection and purchase of new books. This was a very important job because it involved a huge financial outlay. Boots tried its best to give impatient subscribers the new titles they craved but it was a delicate balancing act. A new book could be immensely popular and in huge demand during the first months after publication, then fall from favour. It wouldn't do to buy a large quantity of a title which would soon have to be sold second hand and at a loss. Fiction was most popular with subscribers - mainly light fiction. But the shelves also contained plenty of biographies, travel, history and poetry.

It was important to anticipate trends and tendencies of reading and then forestall them. To this end, Richardson employed panels of experienced readers to sample forthcoming books and report back to him. And he wasn't content with a brief resume. He wanted to know the plot of every novel, what its characters were like, subject content and the quality of the writing.

Richardson was a powerful man, both within the libraries and in the larger world of publishing. A generous order from Boots could establish a book's credibility and greatly influence its chances of success. Kingsley Amis was advised by his publisher, Victor Gollancz, to alter the sentence: "*I feel sorry for that poor bugger*", in his book "That Uncertain Feeling", unless he wanted to risk losing the 2,000 sales to Boots Booklovers Library. Amis lost no time in acquiescing.

For best-selling authors such as Priestley or Walpole, the pre-publication order from Boots might total two thousand copies, with perhaps another five hundred copies to follow later. For less well-known writers, orders from the leading subscription libraries could amount to 25% - 30% of the total print number.

The controversial writer and painter Wyndham Lewis, had a couple of run-ins with Boots because of his earthy language. "The Revenge of Love" was to be entitled "False Bottoms", until Richardson registered his displeasure. In fact, Boots' initial report on the novel was so unfavourable that Cassell threatened to abandon publication altogether. The book deals with communist activity in Spain leading up to the Spanish Civil War, and portrays intellectual English travellers as being hoodwinked and duped. Published in 1937, it was considered by many to be Wyndham Lewis's finest novel.

The inter-war years were tough ones for publishers and orders from circulating libraries such as Boots, Mudie's and W H Smith, helped keep them afloat. Boots alone had half a million subscribers in the 1930s and the success of a novel might owe a great deal to Freddie Richardson's initial opinion of it. Boots' weekly order was a cause for jubilation or despair in any publishing office.

Richardson was well aware of the value of personal recommendation and he shrewdly endeavoured to manipulate this, using the formidable powers at his disposal. He chose his many reading panels with the greatest care and would give them all free copies of pre publication books. These would be provided by the publishers, who would also pay Richardson a fee. Boots' reading teams understood there was an expectation that they would share their opinions of the books they read, with as wide an audience as was feasible and in as encouraging a manner as possible.

Public libraries did not cater for middle class people who wanted to read the latest fashionable book, regardless of merit, or those with an insatiable appetite for light fiction. Boots supplied this need but it did present them with difficulties, mainly ones of expense. In Richardson's view, the main problem was a surfeit of new books being published each year.

He had his own ideas about curtailing production and would have liked to intervene personally, so strongly and in such a way that would result in publishers being compelled to limit output. This demonstrates the high opinion Richardson had of his power and influence in the literary world.

The outbreak of WWII brought different problems for publishers, for circulating libraries and for voracious bookworms. At a time when reading was becoming ever more popular, with people desperate for cheap and home-based pastimes, there were fewer books available, due to the paper shortage.

Freddie Richardson must surely have relished the challenge to devise resourceful solutions to this dilemma and one can only speculate about his possible reluctance to withdraw into the quieter life of an old age pensioner. But willingly or unwillingly, Boots Head Librarian retired from the job in 1941, after thirty years service.

6. THE RULE BOOK

"If there is anything in these regulations which is not perfectly clear, do not hesitate to submit your difficulty to the Head Librarian, who will always be pleased to explain any point which you do not understand or which is not quite clear to you."

Freddie Richardson. Head Librarian

Otherwise known as the Revised Instructional Circular Letters, the book of rules was the creation of Boots Head Librarian, Freddie Richardson.

In 1934, the Rule Book comprised fifty-two pages of detailed instructions. Numbering 206 points, each point was itself often divided into six or more sections. Mr Richardson believed the RICL to be practically infallible, as is made clear in his accompanying letter.

"It is unnecessary for me to stress the value of this production to all Librarians as a guide and reference in the

*working of the Library system and the maintenance of the real live principles of **EFFICIENCY WITH ECONOMY.**"*

All contingencies which could possibly arise during the course of library work were covered in exhaustive detail: *"Suffice it to say that there is scarcely an occasion can happen but that these rules and regulations will put it right."*

There followed just the tiniest hint of menace: *"I hope every Librarian will deem it her duty to make consistent reference thereto, that none may plead ignorance thereof in the performance of their daily work."*

The contents of the Rule Book were top secret: *"I want to impress on all Librarians that this compilation is a matter of internal privacy and confidence and in no circumstances may such either wholly or in part, leave the branch."*

Amongst the plethora of instructions about day-to-day procedures regarding issuing, renewing and cancelling subscriptions, were certain specific directives, which were imperative to the smooth running of the library.

RED LABEL BOOKS

Novels which were considered risqué or likely to cause offence had red labels slapped on their spines, to distinguish them from normal stock. These books were never placed on the open shelves. In fact, they were all kept at library HQ and only sent out to branches when requested by the more daring subscribers, where they were secreted away in the Bespoke Room, awaiting collection.

The Rule Book was very clear in its instructions: *"A red label volume **MUST NOT** be allowed on the shelves and after* *return by the subscriber for whom the book was ordered,* **MUST** *be immediately returned to HQ. The title* **MUST NOT** *be recommended to subscribers."*

"Lady Chatterley's Lover" by D.H. Lawrence would most certainly have been a Red Label Book, if indeed Boots purchased the 1932 edition, published by Martin Secker. The unexpurgated version was not available in the UK until the Penguin publication in 1960, when 200,000 copies were sold on the first day of publication.

INFECTED VOLUMES

Notifiable diseases during the 1930s included measles, whooping cough, poliomyelitis, smallpox, scarlet fever, plague, typhus, diphtheria and erysipelas. In England and Wales at this time, diphtheria was among the top three causes of death for children under fifteen years of age, so fear of contagious disease was well founded

Leading doctors, Sanitary Authorities and the Medical Board of Health, all believed that books could never be satisfactorily disinfected. Boots took the matter so seriously that The Rule Book required a total of three pages and forty itemised points to adequately cover it. *"For the protection of all our subscribers and in the interest of our own reputation, it is essential that the definite and stringent rules laid down to govern the procedure regarding Infected Volumes, should be observed."*

There was nothing half hearted about the measures, which were taken. *"It is our invariable practice to destroy by* **FIRE** *or cause to be destroyed by the local Medical Officer, all books which have been in an infected area."* Books were incinerated even if there was only the faintest suspicion they had been contaminated.

Boots needed library users to be prompt in reporting exposure to contagion and so endeavoured to encourage openness and honesty. *"We have no desire to profit by the misfortunes of our subscribers and therefore, the cost of replacing all books which it may be considered expedient to destroy, is wholly borne by the Management, no charge being made upon the subscriber whatsoever."*

Nevertheless, there were occasions when customers were suspected of being less than honest. If a Librarian had good reason to believe that one of her subscribers had been in close proximity to infection, she was required to report her suspicions to Freddie Richardson and await instructions.

But she was warned to be very certain of her facts. *"This is a delicate matter and one which requires careful handling, for if the report should prove to be without sufficient foundation, subscribers would naturally resent the imputation."*

Some customers' occupations were riskier than others. *"Should any nurses, matrons or other persons connected with Hospitals or Public Health Institutions, desire to take out a subscription, they should be requested to furnish a written guarantee that none of our books or magazines will come into contact with any infectious disease."*

When condemned books were returned to the library, staff had to parcel them up and return them to HQ, in a package with INFECTED VOLUMES clearly marked on the outside. There was also a question and answer form to complete and return but... *"The Q&A reporting infection should **NOT**"* *be packed with the volumes returned, as the entire parcel is destroyed upon receipt, without opening."*

WATCHING THE PENNIES

Boots Booklovers Library was never expected to make a huge profit. It's raison d'être was to encourage a more affluent class of customer into the shops and, hopefully, to make a few extra sales as well.

But the Head Librarian was not a man to be satisfied with achieving the minimum standards required of him. And he expected library staff to share his lofty goals. In particular, he required them to be vigilant and constantly on the lookout for any customers who were abusing the system.

"Where a librarian has reason to believe that a subscriber is in possession of more books than subscribed for, notification should be sent to the Head Librarian immediately. In these cases, Librarians must be most careful that the customer is not allowed to suspect that we mistrust the correct use of the subscription."

The On Demand service was unique to Boots, guaranteeing the supply of any book (if in print) within three days. Class A subscribers expected to be regularly supplied with new titles. This service was expensive and library managers were required to complete forms alerting HQ about popular titles which were falling out of favour with the public, so that no more copies would be bought. *"**THIS IS A MOST IMPORTANT DUTY AND REQUIRES THE UTMOST CARE.** Any inaccuracy is deemed **A VERY SERIOUS MATTER** since purchases are made by HQ on the information given."*

Negligence would appear to be potentially a sacking offence. *"Where a check reveals carelessness, the Senior*

Librarian will be required to give an explanation which if not deemed satisfactory, will necessitate drastic action."

PERKS OF THE JOB

Library staff were encouraged to read widely and familiarise themselves with the stock, primarily in order to help subscribers choose books. But - as might be expected - strict boundaries were applied. *"No employee of the firm, with the exception of the Permanent Library Staff, is permitted the free use of the Boots Booklovers Library."*

"Free" was not really the appropriate word. Library staff were offered modest reductions in both Class A and Class B categories of subscription. *"These terms only apply where the subscription is for the actual personal use of the subscriber. Books taken out must not be used outside the subscribers' own household. Failure to comply with these conditions will result in the withdrawal of the privilege."*

Mr Richardson's parsimonious imagination tormented him with all manner of ways in which a devious library assistant might infringe the Rules, thereby depriving the management of a few pence. *"We understand that it has been and is the practice at some branches for assistants to temporarily borrow (without payment) library books and magazines, to read during meal times, both on and off the premises. This practice is entirely wrong and any infraction of the rule must be reported to HQ."*

Boots relied on regular book sales to recoup much of their financial outlay. These sales were popular both with subscribers and the general public. Books which were no longer in a pristine state or of which there were multiple copies, due to a short period of intense popularity, were offered for sale and advertised in special brochures. "*The Periodical Guide and Monthly Record are useful to those of your subscribers who are customary book buyers. Therein are shown the newest books which will be withdrawn from circulation and available for sale in due course.*"

Library staff were granted a reduction on some of these books. "*A discount is permitted to the staff of 2d in the shilling on book sale volumes of 1/6d and over. Under 1s 6d, a discount is **NOT** allowed.*"

In 1939, one of the books listed for sale at four shillings was "Arms and the Covenant" by Winston Churchill. Originally published in 1938 and purchased by Boots for eighteen shillings, this book contained forty-one of the great man's passionate speeches, warning of the Nazi menace:

"*For five years I have talked to the House on these matters... I have watched this famous island descending incontinently, fecklessly, the stairway which leads to a dark gulf. It is a fine broad stairway at the beginning, but after a bit the carpet ends. A little farther on there are only flagstones, and a little farther on still these break beneath your feet... if mortal catastrophe should overtake the British Nation and the British Empire, historians a thousand years hence will still be baffled... They will never understand how it was that a victorious nation... suffered themselves to be brought low, and to cast away all that they had gained.*"

Another title, listed for sale in the same year at 3s 6d, was a book called "Germany Speaks." Published in London by Thornton Butterworth in May 1938 for 10s 6d, this attempted to put an acceptable face on the activities of Nazi Germany. Walter Gross, head of the Reich Bureau for Enlightenment on Population Policy and Racial Welfare, contributed a chapter. He argued that: *"unrestrained propagation among the hereditarily unfit, the mentally deficient, imbeciles and hereditary criminals, etc had led to a birth rate nine times greater than that of the fitter inhabitants."*

KEEPING A WATCHFUL EYE

"It is of great importance that all volumes should be carefully examined when handed in by subscribers and any damage to same must be tactfully brought to their notice at the time."

Damage to the cover of a book was immediately obvious and could be dealt with by means of an "on the spot" charge. i.e. 1s 9d for large books and 1s 6d for fiction.

Staff were expected to swiftly examine each book on its return, checking for damage or defilement. In the event of torn or stained pages being discovered, the matter was brought to the attention of the subscriber and no doubt many a difficult conversation ensued. The damaged book was then returned to HQ, where an invoice would be issued and the subscriber asked to pay up on their next visit to the library.

Some customers - probably even refined readers of the LADY - were not to be trusted: *"Particular care should be taken to see that magazines are not surreptitiously removed from the magazine table, while the librarian is engaged on other duties."*

TIDY HOUSE TIDY MIND

Junior staff were expected to dust books every morning before the library opened and the Rule Book stressed the importance of this task. *"The care of stock at a branch is one of the most important duties of a librarian. The books on the shelves should be regularly and systematically dusted and all volumes showing a worn or dilapidated appearance should be turned out and forwarded to HQ."*

The library was expected to present a neat and attractive appearance at all times. *"Librarians should never hold at the branch more stock than the shelves can accommodate, for there is **nothing** that presents a more untidy appearance than volumes stacked elsewhere than on shelves."*

Boots were fortunate to have Freddie Richardson as their Head Librarian for thirty years. Highly intelligent and a stickler for detail, his absolute commitment to the company was indisputable. In particular, he was an astute businessman, with his finger on every penny.

The character of the man is revealed on every page of his Rule Book. Meticulous, pedantic, bossy - not someone to suffer fools gladly. But perhaps he was unaware that he might possibly be viewed as a somewhat formidable authority figure.

His intention was certainly to appear approachable. *"If there is anything in these regulations which is not perfectly clear, do not hesitate to submit your difficulty to the Head Librarian, who will always be pleased to **explain any point which you do not understand or which is not quite clear to you.**"*

Presumably some brave souls even took him up on his offer.

7. EXAMINATION DAY

"Many women subscribers prefer not to be bothered by too much deduction and find such writers as Dorothy Sayers and Ngaio Marsh, too exacting for them."

Examiner's revision notes. Circa 1947

Junior staff received extensive training and sat Boots library exams, which covered the Boots circulating system, service to subscribers and book knowledge. Guidance notes were distributed to candidates several weeks beforehand, to enable thorough preparation and revision. These included specific advice from the Examiner. We don't know his name but aspects of his personality are tantalisingly revealed in his Helpful Hints, probably written sometime in the late 1940s.

CRIME

For test purposes, books in this popular genre were classed as either detectives or thrillers, although the Examiner did admit that deciding where a book belonged was not always an easy task. Guidance notes advised that a good mystery spanned all tastes, ranged from highbrow to lowbrow and was enjoyed by almost everyone. Literary value was not the deciding factor, so long as Booklovers were given a few hours of agreeable escapism. 1913 - 1953 is generally considered the Golden Age of detective fiction.

QUEEN BEES OF CRIME

Dorothy L Sayers was classed as one of the "Queens of Crime", alongside Agatha Christie, Ngaio Marsh and Marjorie Allingham. Her books were definitely detective stories and featured her amateur sleuth, Lord Peter Wimsey. Mr Examiner could find no fault with this Queen Bee. *"Dorothy Sayers enjoys a reputation for thoroughness and accuracy in detail and she always presents us with interesting background to her stories."*

Ngaio Marsh was a New Zealander, whose books star Inspector Roderick Alleyn, a gentleman detective working for the Metropolitan Police. Like Lord Peter Wimsey, he is well bred, charming and intelligent. Ngaio Marsh also earns top marks from Mr E. *"This writer usually introduces her characters and reveals her plot for the reader to form a conclusion and test it with the solution of the detective. The idea of family scandals is an essential part of her theme."*

Marjorie Allingham produced her first crime novel in 1928 and continued writing for forty years. She regarded the mystery novel as a box with four sides - a killing, a mystery, an enquiry and a conclusion with an element of satisfaction in it. Her detective was Albert Campion, aristocratic, unassuming, mild and bespectacled. Agatha Christie said that Marjorie Allingham stood out like a shining light. Mr E's appraisal is succinct: *"Excellent detective stories with a flavour of romance."*

Dame Agatha Mary Clarissa Christie DBE is the most widely published author of all time, outsold only by the Bible and Shakespeare. Her books have sold over a billion copies in the English language alone. She wrote eighty crime novels and short story collections and her protagonists, Hercule Poirot and Jane Marple have remained popular and well loved for almost a century.

Pat Oldale remembers foreign students in Bournemouth being encouraged to read Agatha Christie's books because they were well written in excellent English. Mr Examiner could only pay tribute to Mrs Christie's lofty status. *"The most popular of all present day mystery writers, with an entirely general appeal. Her secret is the ability to tell a yarn in a simple, easy way."*

POPULAR BUT LESS EXALTED DETECTIVE FICTION

Mr E confided that he once had a lady subscriber who was tired of Mills and Boon fiction and wanted to move on to something a little more challenging. He suggested the novels of Patricia Wentworth. In his opinion, her books contained just the right amount of excitement to relieve the ordinary love story, while still including an element of romance: *"Many women subscribers prefer not to be bothered by too much deduction and find such writers as Dorothy Sayers and Ngaio Marsh, too exacting for them."*

Other writers who fell into the category of blending a satisfying amount of romance and mystery, narrated in a light manner, were Ann Hocking, M.G Eberhart and Ethel Lena White. This last writer was best known for her novel "The Wheel Spins", published in 1936 and on which the Alfred Hitchcock film "The Lady Vanishes", was based.

Mr E moved swiftly on to male subscribers who: *"Often cannot be bothered by psychology or romance and prefer their detective stories neat."* In his opinion, one outstanding writer guaranteed to appeal to most men was Austin Freeman. A doctor by profession, Freeman used his practical experience to unfold the science of criminology. His detective, Dr Thorndyke, was usually found surrounded by test tubes, forceps and microscopes: *"He is the only fictional detective whose methods have been put into use by real police."*

Mr E suggested recommending to those subscribers who enjoyed clever, well written detective stories, any books published by Messrs Gollancz: *"A firm who have acquired quite a reputation in this respect. You will find among their authors, such writers as Michael Innes, Edmund Crispin, Ellery Queen and H.P. Knox."*

LIGHT ROMANCES

Mr E began by telling candidates that this paper was concerned with books generally enjoyed by women subscribers: *"They often take their literature of relaxation in a gentler form than men do and prefer tales of romance or about families. We often hear them say they like a 'pretty book'. I am sure your taste in reading has developed far above this level but it is our duty to supply books to our subscribers without questioning their taste."*

Sensation novels became hugely popular in late 19th century England, just before the formation of Boots Booklovers Library. They focused on shocking subject matter, including adultery, theft, kidnapping, insanity, bigamy, forgery, seduction and murder. Many titles became immediate best sellers on publication, surpassing all previous book sales records.

Mrs Henry Wood was a particularly successful writer of the Victorian era. The most famous of her books was "East Lynne", published in 1861. Although moral in tone, this is no innocent escapade. The story overflows with scandal and is drenched in adultery, lust, sadism and masochism. It belongs to the sensational class of novel eagerly welcomed by Victorian ladies, bored to tears in the suffocating world of middle class domesticity. The much quoted line "*Dead! Dead! And never called me Mother*!" is from the stage version of "East Lynne" and does not appear in the book.

Marie Corelli was the undisputed literary superstar of the late 19th century. With her book "The Sorrows of Satan", she broke all previous publishing records and boasted Queen Victoria amongst her fans. Mr E shows a degree of reluctant respect for this staggeringly successful writer. "*I am sure there are still some of Miss Corelli's admirers subscribing to our library who wonder what has happened to their old favourite. I know it is often difficult to please our elderly ladies because they do not understand that all literature moves with the times and our present day authors cannot supply quite the same material.*"

Mr E attributed to Ethel M Dell the accolade of being the writer from whose books the successful love story evolved. He said her formula went as follows:

1) The *hero is strong and silent. The strength applies to his physique and the silence to a rather dour temperament. He usually comes from a good family but owing to some misunderstanding, has cut himself off from society to brood in the outposts of the Empire.*

2) The *heroine is very well bred indeed, possessing a distant, ethereal sort of beauty. She has been so delicately nurtured, that she finds it imperative to find someone to lean on.*

3) By *some strange streak of fate, these two opposites meet. At first, she is repulsed by the brute but gradually her delicate charm brings forth a softer side to his nature and they become mutually attracted to each other. After one or two skirmishes with fate, they abolish their differences and the story ends with a fervent embrace."*

Ethel M Dell's readers adored her novels but critics hated them, taking pleasure in counting the number of times she used such words as Passion, Tremble, Pant and Thrill. Her heroes were proud, aloof, withdrawn and in need of taming. But they were also passionate, loyal, forceful and usually rich. A heady blend of attributes and bound to lead to discontent amongst women obliged to make do with a far more humdrum sort of chap. This poem written by A.P. Herbert, encapsulates it admirably:

"Jack loves me well enough, I know,

But does he ever bite his lip,

And does he chew his cheek to show

That Passion's got him in a grip?

An' does his gun go pop-pop-pop-

When fellers get familiar?   No.

He just says, 'Op it!" and they 'op-

It may be life, but ain't it slow?"

"Elinor Glyn and E.M. Hull introduced into their novels, a more daring spirit of freedom", says Mr E, carefully ambiguous. In fact, Ethel Maud Hull produced the nearest thing to pornography ever written by any of the inter-war female novelists.

Published in 1919, "The Sheik" is the story of an English girl who is kidnapped in the desert by an Arabian Sheik. After he has brutally raped her over a period of months, she finally decides that she has fallen in love with him.

Elinor Glyn, another writer of early 20th century erotica, endorses inexplicable female behaviour of this sort. In her view, a woman would stand almost anything from a passionate lover. Elinor Glyn's most famous novel, entitled "Three Weeks" and published in 1907, had sold five million copies by the early 1930s.

This was the story of a clandestine affair between an Englishman and a mysterious older woman, who he knows only as The Lady. The most sensual scene, which made Elinor Glyn famous, took place in a foreign location on a tiger skin. It inspired the following doggerel:

"Would you like to sin with Elinor Glyn on a tiger skin?

Or would you prefer to err with her on some other fur?"

These sexual scenes of abandon usually occurred somewhere remote and exotic and in this way could be disassociated from respectable British behaviour. The circulating libraries used this as a flimsy excuse for continuing to buy the scandalous books their subscribers craved.

Mr E dealt briskly with the popularity of both Elinor Glyn and E.M. Hull: "This was the sort of book which girls read surreptitiously when it was first published but nowadays it seems so innocuous and silly that it is disregarded entirely."

He might be disconcerted to know that both "Three Weeks" and "The Sheik", were reprinted in the 1960s by Virago Modern Classics and can still be found, buried deep within the archives of public libraries.

FAMILY STORIES

The female Boots Booklover tended to move on to family stories when the bland diet of light romance started to pall. She often requested a "well written book" but Mr Examiner warned staff against taking this too literally. *"These subscribers are certainly not in the frame of mind to accept the analytical studies of - say - Aldous Huxley or Virginia Woolf and would even fight shy of Priestley or Frances Brett Young. All they want is an easy story, which contains some reality instead of the make believe of which they are tired. They are ready to receive the works of a writer able to give a simple picture of characters which do bear some resemblance to the people we meet every day and the book which would interest most, would be one which depicts a family."*

After some consideration, Mr E eliminated "The Herb of Grace" by Elizabeth Goudge. Although the content was suitable *"the bulk might possibly frighten a reader who is used to the very lightest material."*

Some books, such as those written by Ursula Bloom, he regarded as midway between the love story and the family tale, so could be confidently recommended to a subscriber attempting to wean herself off Ethel M Dell.

Once certain that a customer was comfortable with the works of Ms Bloom, the library assistant could gently lead the way into the realms of slightly more demanding fiction. *"Something a degree heavier and longer,"* Mr E suggested. *"D.E. Stevenson perhaps, or Marjorie Sharp, Rose Franken and those of Doris Leslie's which are not historical. After a woman has acquired a taste for these, she will soon be prepared to accept greater length. Perhaps the novels of Dorothy Whipple."*

Dorothy Whipple was an extremely successful writer, who lived in Nottingham for most of her married life. She wrote for women like herself who were intelligent, with an acute sense of justice but fundamentally loving and committed to family life. Her book "They Were Sisters", published in 1943, is deceptively gentle in tone but centres on the disturbing theme of domestic violence in the Thirties.

In this novel, Dorothy Whipple depicts the low status of middleclass women in British Society, at a time when an ordinary woman would find it almost impossible to free herself from a violent husband. To quote one of the sisters: *"It was monstrous that such a man as Geoffrey should have such power but there was no appeal against it."*

Mr E believed that women negotiating the journey between light romance and family story, needed to be coaxed, sensitively encouraged and not exposed to anything too taxing. *"It is wise to avoid any form of regional dialect if possible, unless it applies to the particular district you serve, for at this stage of development the reader is not prepared to accept anything unfamiliar and the people she is concerned with must use her own language."*

When her subscriber has acquired sufficient confidence to saunter past the Mills and Boon and onwards to those shelves containing family stories, the young Boots library assistant can feel all the satisfaction of a job well done. *"If handled with delicate understanding, you will soon find that these subscribers will develop from what we may describe as "lowbrow" to "middlebrow" readers. Their minds will soon become receptive to new ideas and your field of possible recommendations will become far wider."*

TOPICAL EVENTS AND CURRENT AFFAIRS

There were a huge number of books published about topical events in the first half of the 20th century and they included both fiction and non-fiction. *"This is the type of book which usually enjoys a short but spectacular career,"* said Mr E. *"While a subject is fresh in the minds of people, they flock to read about it but when something new appears, it is easily pushed aside and forgotten."*

With memories of two World Wars very much in the forefront of people's minds, many books had been written, attempting to explain and understand the recent past. *"Time will sort out the most significant books of the day but it might be interesting to look back upon some of the factors which have influenced both writers and readers since the 1920's."*

The Depression and unemployment opened up new realms of literature, featuring economic hardship and impoverished social conditions. In 1933, Walter Greenwood wrote "Love on the Dole", a book about working class poverty in Lancashire. This was followed a couple of years later by A J. Cronin's "The Stars Look Down", which centred on the difficult and dangerous lives led by members of a North country coal mining family.

Then in 1936, the Royal family grabbed the headlines with the abdication of King Edward VIII. *"The historical significance of this event remains to be proved," Mr E cautioned, "but several writers took the opportunity of writing about it at the time; the most notable being Compton Mackenzie, who published an historical background of the Royal family called "The Windsor Tapestry."*

In spite of the shortage of paper and manpower in the printing trade, there were an exceptional number of books published in the 1940s, of which the majority were related to the war in some way.

Richard Dimbleby, the BBC's representative in the Middle East, recounted his experiences in "The Frontiers are Green". Many men spent all their spare time in the Home Guard and John Brophy documented this in the highly popular "Britain's Home Guard".

Women's wartime role was also recognised. In "No Time For Tears" published in 1944, Margaret Sherman recounts her experiences in the ATS. The book contains a foreword by Dame Regina Evans, Chief Commander of the ATS.

The Auxiliary Territorial Service was the women's branch of the British Army during WWII. It was formed on 9th September 1938, initially as a women's voluntary service. In 1949 the ATS was merged into the Women's Royal Army Corps.

Richard Hillary was a Battle of Britain pilot who was killed in 1943, soon after the publication of his book "The Last Enemy." Mr E believed this to be one of the finest pieces of literature produced during WWII. *"This very poignant autobiography of a young airman who suffered both mentally and physically, epitomises the nature and the spirit of the young men who fought in the Battle of Britain. In the same way that the poet Rupert Brooke, who was killed in 1915, typified the young men of the first world war, does Richard Hillary represent those who followed in WWII."*

By 1944, although the war dragged on, people were becoming increasingly reluctant to read about battles and fighting. *"Those of you who were librarians during these years will remember that war books were very popular for a time. But people grew very tired of them towards the end of hostilities and turned for comfort to experiences other than their own."*

Despite the growing public distaste for books about conflict, some continued to be best-sellers for several years. Amongst these was "The Gathering Storm" by Winston Churchill, "The Wooden Horse" by Eric Williams and "The Purple Plain" by H.E. Bates. All these titles were based upon wartime experiences.

"I have tried, in this paper, to give examples of books which arise to meet the need of the moment. Although the majority usually fade into obscurity, it is important to remember that they serve a purpose by making people aware of what is going on around them and often help to elucidate some of the problems which arise from day to day."

JUVENILE SUBSCRIBERS

In the late 1940s, libraries were cautiously beginning to welcome children but this did not meet with universal approval. It was an era when many people could still remember - and perhaps wistfully recall - the days when libraries were regarded as being adult only establishments. Children had no option but to read the books chosen for them by their parents and these tended to be worthwhile and dull, rather than exciting and enjoyable.

In Boots, all children were class B subscribers, which simplified matters. But Mr E reminded staff that they must be treated with the same consideration as adult readers. *"If a librarian has the right approach towards children, she will find they can be easily trained to be model subscribers. The possession of a library token with their name upon it means a great deal to children and makes them feel grown up. We must remember never to talk down to these independent youngsters; they like things explained in clear, simple language without any hint of condescension."*

Children wanted to be left alone to choose their own books because that was part of the fun of belonging to a library. But sometimes a little guidance was appreciated. *"It takes very little time to help them and the service you perform will leave a lasting impression."*

Left to themselves, children do tend to become a little noisy but Mr E favoured as much leniency as possible. *"It may not be wise to encourage them to talk either too loudly or too long but a little conversation is natural even among our "grown up" subscribers and it should not be difficult to explain to the little ones where to draw the line."*

Children were heard to describe whimsical books as "lovely" and adventurous ones as "smashing". Captain W.E. Johns, the creator of Biggles, was particularly popular. His recipe for success was fairly fundamental: *"I teach a boy to be a man, for without that essential qualification he will never be anything. I teach that decent behaviour wins in the end as a natural order of things. I teach the spirit of team work, loyalty to the Crown, the Empire and rightful authority."*

The quality most essential in adventure stories was toughness, announced Mr E. *"If you wish to please a schoolboy, you may rest assured that if you find a book containing a sentence such as "Cedric swept three of them aside and punched another on the jaw", you are on the right track."*

The school story is a form of literature peculiar to the UK because it derives from the British institution of the Public Schools. The first of these books was "Tom Brown's Schooldays", followed by Grey Friars and Billy Bunter.

Angela Brazil was the first author to write school stories for girls. However, she was regarded as rather old fashioned after the war and was swiftly and thoroughly overtaken by the best selling and prolific Enid Blyton. Many a young girl dreamed of going to a boarding school exactly like Malory Towers, glamorously located on the desolate Cornish cliffs. Wistful thirteen year olds yearned to score goals at lacrosse, play tricks on Mam'zelle and scoff tinned sardines and ginger cake at forbidden midnight feasts.

Careers guidance at this time took the form of novels, in which the main character was usually a girl. The focus tended to be on traditional female careers. Heroines worked hard during their training and took job prospects seriously but there was always the assumption of eventual domesticity. Libraries bought large quantities of these books and publishers took great care to ensure that the contents were unlikely to upset parents or teachers.

Hundreds of girls were influenced by the Sue Barton stories written by Helen Dore Boylston, in which she traces the life of a nurse from probationer to superintendent. The first of these books was written in 1936 and the series was significant in providing role models for girls looking for careers, right through the 1930s and into the 1950s. They were highly successful, selling millions of copies and were praised for their authentic representation of nursing practice and freedom from sentimentality. *"It is claimed that these books have brought more recruits to the nursing profession than any of the eulogies upon Florence Nightingale,"* Mr E declared.

The "Cherry Ames" books, written by Helen Wells and Julie Campbell, were mystery novels with hospital settings published between 1943 and 1968. Another book based on a career in medicine - this time for boys - was "Students at Queen's" by John Stuart Arey.

Peter Dawlish was another writer who produced books for boys. He wrote a careers story series about the Merchant Navy. "The First Tripper" follows a cadet through his initial sea voyage to Alexandria and Australia. This identifies the qualities and temperament required to cope with the tribulations of life as a junior member of the crew.

But so far as imaginative story telling was concerned, Arthur Ransome vied with Enid Blyton for first place in children's affections. "Swallows and Amazons" is a book with enduring appeal for adventurous youngsters. *"It exercises their energy and imagination in practical ways. They hammer, paint, cook, navigate and swab decks. They employ themselves with such gusto to the make believe of being grownup and self reliant, that they have no time for quarrels or personal difficulties.*

Mr E well knew that people will always remember with affection those books which stirred their youthful imaginations, enabling them to escape into worlds of unlimited adventure, friendship and fun. *"I am sure if we can help our young subscribers enjoy their reading, they will never forget the pleasure they obtained from the Boots Booklovers Library and consequently remain subscribers and customers when they grow up."*

This prediction was entirely accurate, as is proved by the many former subscribers who retain affectionate childhood memories of the first books they borrowed. Josephine Walker remembers her Boots library on Fishergate in Preston, Lancashire. The very first book she borrowed was "Veronica at the Wells", by Lorna Hill. Josephine recalls a luxurious, magical library setting, richly carpeted and with wood panelling. She can still visualise the librarian sitting behind an imposing oak desk, with a leather top and says the atmosphere was opulent but also cosy and welcoming - with a wonderland quality about it.

8. A BAKER'S DOZEN: BOOKLOVERS FAVOURITE READS IN THE GLORY DAYS

"Men are simpler than you imagine my sweet child. But what goes on in the twisted, tortuous minds of women would baffle anyone."

Daphne Du Maurier "Rebecca"

SEVEN PILLARS OF WISDOM by T.E. Lawrence. Published 1935

"All men dream: but not equally. Those who dream by night in the dusty recesses of their minds wake up in the day to find it was vanity, but the dreamers of the day are dangerous men, for they may act their dreams with open eyes, to make it possible."

"I loved you, so I drew these tides of men into my hands and wrote my will across the sky in stars."

"He was old and wise, which meant tired and disappointed..."

T E Lawrence poured his soul into this outstanding autobiography, published immediately following his death. It takes the reader from his arrival in Cairo as an upstart academic, through his dramatic evolution into a desert soldier, strategist and leader of the Arab revolt against the Turks, to his ultimate failure to win justice for the people he'd grown to be part of. In Winston Churchill's opinion, as a narrative of war and adventure, the book is unsurpassable. John Buchan declared that although he was not normally much of a hero worshipper, he could have followed T.E. Lawrence over the edge of the world.

GONE WITH THE WIND by Margaret Mitchell. Published 1936

"Well, my dear, take heart. Some day, I will kiss you and you will like it. But not now, so I beg you not to be too impatient."

"Now she had a fumbling knowledge that, had she ever understood Ashley, she would never have loved him; had she ever understood Rhett, she would never have lost him."

"How closely women clutch the very chains that bind them!"

"Death and taxes and childbirth! There's never a convenient time for any of them!"

"I want to make you faint. I will make you faint. You've had this coming to you for years. None of the fools you've known have kissed you like this - have they? Your precious Charles or Frank or your stupid Ashley... I said Your Stupid Ashley. Gentlemen all - what do they know about women? What do they know about you? I know you."

"I wish I could care what you do or where you go but I can't. My dear, I don't give a damn."

Scarlett O'Hara is a woman who can survive anything: the American Civil War, Atlanta burning, the Union Army looting her beloved Tara and even the carpetbaggers who pounce greedily on what little she has left. Scarlett is beautiful, feisty, passionate and she's in love with the wrong man - the wrong married man but that little complication only serves to fan the flames of her obsession.

This is the epic tale of a woman who claws and fights her way through one of the most turbulent and dangerous periods in American history. The tough and ruthless Scarlett vows never to be poor and hungry again, no matter what it takes, even if that means callously seducing and marrying her sister's boyfriend.

Scarlett is selfish, snobbish, heartless, a false friend and a dreadful mother. But she is also brave, enterprising, energetic and captivating, qualities which are demonstrated in the courage she shows as she fights to survive, during and after the war.

But her blinkered adoration of a weak man is infuriating and her inability to understand or value Rhett's love is frustrating and ultimately tragic. *"Tomorrow I'll think of some way to get him back,"* Scarlett vows, gutsy as ever. But the reader knows that the game is up and Rhett Butler has gone for good. It serves her right and yet how we yearn for a happy ending.

THE CITADEL by A.J. Cronin. Published 1937

"You are very attractive. And your greatest charm is that you do not realise it."

"I have written in **"The Citadel"** *all I feel about the medical profession,"* Cronin stated, when interviewed. *"Its injustices, its hide-bound unscientific stubbornness, its humbug ... the horrors and inequities detailed in the story, I have personally witnessed. This is not an attack against individuals but against a system."*

This is the tale of the idealistic Doctor Andrew Manson, who starts off working in the mining towns of the South Wales valleys, before being lured into the world of fashionable London doctors. In the valleys, Manson fought the diseases of poverty, including poor housing conditions and industrial injuries. In London he encounters the hypochondria of the idle rich, for whom his fellow physicians cynically prescribe quack treatments, swiftly followed by inflated bills. His marriage is in crisis and during a separation from his wife Manson has an affair, which he deeply regrets.

A few of the more vociferous medical practitioners of the day took exception to one of the book's many messages; that a few well-heeled doctors in fashionable practices were ripping off their affluent patients. The majority accepted it for what it was - a perceptive, topical novel.

REBECCA by Daphne Du Maurier. Published 1938

"Last night I dreamt I went to Manderley again."

"I am glad it cannot happen twice, the fever of first love. For it is a fever, and a burden, too, whatever the poets may say."

"It wouldn't make for sanity would it, living with the devil."

"Men are simpler than you imagine my sweet child. But what goes on in the twisted, tortuous minds of women would baffle anyone."

The nameless narrator of Rebecca is shy and socially inept. In Monte Carlo she falls in love with the handsome, inscrutable Maximilian de Winter. An air of mystery clings to him. He is a man on the run, desperate to escape the shadows of the past, the memories and associations of his beautiful Cornish house, Manderley. He proposes marriage and the narrator accepts. They return to Manderley and the ghosts of de Winter's past.

The house hides dark secrets, all of which concern Max's first wife, Rebecca. Manderley is as much an atmosphere as a tangible erection of stones and mortar. Both house and novel acquire a dream-like quality. Into this steps the nightmarish figure of Mrs Danvers, gothic housekeeper and fanatical protector of Rebecca's memory. Mrs Danvers unsettles the second Mrs de Winter, who finds herself overwhelmed by Manderley - its grandeur, its ambience, its personnel and most of all, its master, whose behaviour here seems so remote, so changed.

Agatha Christie earned Daphne Du Maurier's indignation by echoing the question so many readers had asked: why does the narrator have no name? Perhaps she was better pleased by reports that Neville Chamberlain was reading Rebecca, when he flew to Munich to meet Hitler in 1939. The novel's wartime associations did not stop there. Field Marshal Rommel kept a copy of Rebecca at his headquarters. Although ultimately it would not be used, the Nazis mined Rebecca as the source for a code for German agents infiltrating Cairo.

HOW GREEN WAS MY VALLEY by Richard Llewellyn. Published 1939

"O, there is lovely to feel a book, a good book, firm in the hand, for its fatness holds rich promise, and you are hot inside to think of good hours to come."

"I saw my father as a man, and not as a man who was my father."

"I am Angharad Morgan," she said, and the river never ran colder.   "Go to hell."

"Everywhere was singing, all over the house was singing, and outside the house was alive with singing, and the very air was song."

Richard Llewellyn claimed to have been born in St David's, Pembrokeshire, Wales. After his death, it was revealed that although his parents were Welsh, his birthplace was Hendon in Middlesex.

The Morgans are a poor but respectable mining family in the South Wales valleys. Their story is told through the eyes of the youngest son, Huw Morgan. Huw's academic prowess sets him apart from his brothers and enables him to contemplate a future away from this troubled industrial environment.

Huw's sister Angharad falls in love with the local minister but circumstances conspire to keep them apart and she marries the son of a wealthy mine owner. When the marriage falls apart and she returns to the village, rumours of a liaison between her and the preacher fuel gossip amongst the scandalmongers.

The novel is saturated with loss and bereavement, beginning with the death of Huw's brother Ivor, in a mining accident. Work becomes scarce, wages are cut and the family is at loggerheads because Mr Morgan gives his support to the mine owners, while his sons want to strike. Eventually Huw's parents watch their surviving sons leave Wales in search of a better life.

FOR WHOM THE BELL TOLLS by Ernest Hemingway. Published 1940

"The world is a fine place and worth fighting for and I hate very much to leave it."

"If you stop complaining and asking for what you never will get, you will have a good life. A good life is not measured by any biblical span."

"There are many who do not know they are fascists but will find it out when the time comes."

"Do you know how an ugly woman feels? Do you know what it is to be ugly all your life and inside to feel that you are beautiful? It is very rare."

"He was violating the second rule of the two rules for getting on well with people who speak Spanish; give the men tobacco and leave the women alone."

This novel of the Spanish Civil War, which takes place over just three or four days, is packed with blood, lust, adventure, comedy and tragedy. The young American, Robert Jordan, is neither a professing Communist nor a professional soldier but an idealistic college tutor, in Spain on sabbatical leave. He joins a guerrilla band operating from a cave high on the Sierra de Guadarrama and is instructed to blow up a bridge, in order to halt the enemy's progress.

Jordan falls in love with Maria, a frightened young peasant girl, whose hair was shaved off by enemy troops, after they shot her parents and rampaged through her native town. Pablo, the guerrillas' perpetually inebriated leader, resents Jordan's attentions toward Maria, and he refuses to help the American in his sabotage work. Pablo's wife Pilar, tough, blasphemous and unattractive, takes over command of the guerrillas and helps Jordan to arrange horses for the gang's departure after the job is done. But the man supplying the horses is killed, and Jordan is left to finish his task without an escape plan.

RANDOM HARVEST by James Hilton. Published 1941

"Have you ever been going somewhere with a crowd and you're certain it's the wrong road and you tell them, but they won't listen, so you just have to plod along in what you know is the wrong direction till somebody more important gets the same idea?"

"It's a very remarkable story." "Remarkable's a well-chosen word. It doesn't give you away."

"There's only one thing more important... and that is, after you've done what you set out to do, to feel that it's been worth doing."

A veteran's comfortable life is thrown into turmoil, when long-buried memories of his time in the trenches of World War I come rushing back. Charles Rainier's family feared him lost, along with so many of Britain's youth during the Great War.

But two years after he was reported missing in action, he appears in a Liverpool hospital with no memory of his missing years. Even after marriage and a life of relative success, he can't recall his time on the battlefield - until the first bombs of the Second World War begin to fall.

Suddenly, his memories flood back. Recollections of a violent battlefield, a German prison, and a passionate affair, all threaten to fracture the peaceful life he has worked so hard to create.

THE PIED PIPER by Nevil Shute. Published 1942

"When you are tired there is pleasure in a conversation taken in sips, like old brandy."

"Children always like a whistle, especially if they see it made."

"You can call a sunset by a filthy name, but you do not spoil its beauty."

Pied Piper is the story of John Howard, a retired Englishman who is on holiday in France at the outbreak of WWII. Reluctantly, he agrees to take two British children back to England with him. En route, Howard meets up with five more children who need his help to escape the Nazis. He is also re-united with a French woman named Nicole, the daughter of an old acquaintance. She helps the ill-assorted group reach the coast, and on the way Howard discovers that they share a common grief.

Much of the plot hinges on the frailties of age, of both the very old and the very young. This is the real enemy, the fifth column within the little group. Howard's weak heart, Sheila's sudden fever and Ronnie's heedless English chatter, supply much of the story's tension and each additional child jacks it up a notch, as their progress slows to a crawl.

It is not in Howard's nature to be less than kind and gentle with a child and nor do we want him to be, even though we know that he could reach safety, if he would only get a move on. The old man eventually arrives home in England with his seven charges but he leaves his heart behind in France.

A TREE GROWS IN BROOKLYN by Betty Smith. Published 1943

"The world was hers for the reading."

"Look at everything always as though you were seeing it either for the first or last time: thus is your time on earth filled with glory."

"I hate all those flirty-birty games that women make up. Life's too short. If you ever find a man you love, don't waste time hanging your head and simpering. Go right up to him and say, "I love you. How about getting married?"

The Nolan family lived in the slums of Brooklyn at the turn of the century. Daughter Francie is imaginative, an avid reader and an adroit observer of human nature. She grows up with a sweet, tragic father, a severely realistic mother and an aunt who gives her love too freely.

The young Francie quickly learns the meaning of hunger and the value of a penny. She is her father's child - romantic and hungry for beauty. But she is also her mother's child - deeply practical and a seeker of the truth. Like the Tree of Heaven that grows out of cement or through cellar gratings, resourceful Francie struggles against all the odds to survive and thrive.

Confronted with revelations of poverty and squalor, the middle classes shuddered with genteel revulsion while reading this book but its humour and pathos ensured its immediate success.

FOREVER AMBER by Kathleen Windsor. Published 1944

"If you had better sense you'd have learned by now that nothing thrives so well as wickedness"

"It seemed that up until this moment she had been only half alive."

"They had stopped now and he gave a glance up at the sky, through the trees, as though to see how much time was left. Amber, watching him, was suddenly struck with panic. Now he was going--out again into that great world with its bustle and noise and excitement--and she must stay here. She had a terrible new feeling of loneliness, as if she stood in some solitary corner at a party where she was the only stranger. Those places he had seen, she would never see; those fine things he had done, she would never do. But worst of all she would never see him again."

Abandoned, pregnant and left penniless on the teeming streets of 17th century London, sixteen year old Amber St Clare scrambles - by means of wits, beauty and courage - to the powerful position of Charles II's favourite mistress.

Against a background of the Plague and Great Fire, the reader is introduced to a world of idle fops, ladies of quality, fashionable couples who loathe each other, highwaymen, peddlers and unfortunate old maids with nothing to do but tend the sick and poor.

Throughout several disastrous marriages and assignations, Amber's heart remains faithful to the one man she truly loves and who she can never have.

The book sold over three million copies, probably helped on its way by being banned in the State of Boston for its overt sexuality.

LARK RISE TO CANDLEFORD by Flora Thompson. Published 1945

"When I am dead and in my head

And all my bones are rotten,

Take this book and think of me

And mind I'm not forgotten."

"No, I be-ant expectin' nothin', but I be so yarnin"

"Candleford Green was but a small village and there were fields and meadows and woods all around it. As soon as Laura crossed the doorstep, she could see some of these. But mere seeing from a distance did not satisfy her; she longed to go alone far into the fields and hear the birds singing, the brooks tinkling, and the wind rustling through the corn, as she had when a child. To smell things and touch things, warm earth and flowers and grasses, and to stand and gaze where no one could see her, drinking it all in."

Originally published as three separate titles, this book is a part lyrical, part documentary portrait of the tiny hamlet, Juniper Hill, where the author was born. Flora Thompson's account of life in rural Oxfordshire in the last decades of the 19th century portrays an entire culture still governed by the rising and setting of the sun.

But the old cyclical rhythms are beginning to break up. The village teenagers leave to work in the big houses as before, but come home with unsettling new ideas. The telegraph is dissolving the barriers of time and space between settlements. There is still a Harvest Home and a village Feast Day, but stalls stocked with factory-made sweets are arriving ... life goes on as well as round.

Flora Thompson's recollections of growing up in an Oxfordshire village capture a vanishing world and create an authentic picture of rural working-class life.

THE RIVER by Rumer Godden. Published 1946

"Harriet was silent, thinking, and then she said, "It is too hard to be a person. You don't only have to go on and on. You have to be--" she looked for the word she needed and could not find it. Then, "You have to be tall as well," said Harriet."

"Harriet told her, 'Captain John was so brave. He stayed there in the battle until his leg was shot off.' Victoria's brown eyes rested thoughtfully on Captain John. "Why didn't he stay until the other leg was shot off?" she asked. But he still seemed to like Victoria best."

"So many grown-up people seem to be nothing very much."

The River is a poignant story of childhood in India. Much, although not all of the story, is a tribute to Rumer Godden's own early life. Harriet, on the cusp of womanhood, feels herself to be between two worlds. Her sister is no longer a playmate and her brother is still a child.

Harriet's world is the garden, the house, the servants, Indian festivals, the jute works and the eternal ebb and flow of the river on its journey to the Bay of Bengal. In little over a year, Harriet experiences birth, death, love, loneliness, pain and joy.

She learns some hard and bitter lessons, all the while observing the people around her and her own life, in the context of the trees, the stars and the river.

DIARY OF ANNE FRANK. Published 1947

"I don't think of all the misery, but of the beauty that still remains."

"But feelings can't be ignored, no matter how unjust or ungrateful they seem."

"I wish to go on living even after my death."

Anne Frank and her family moved from Germany to Amsterdam in 1933, the year the Nazis gained control of Germany. By the beginning of 1940, they were trapped in Amsterdam by the Nazi occupation of the Netherlands. Jewish persecution increased and in 1942 the family went into hiding in the annexe of an old office building.

Cut off from the outside world, they faced hunger, boredom, the relentless pressure of living in confined quarters and the constant threat of discovery and death. Two years later, their whereabouts were betrayed to the Gestapo and they were transported to concentration camps.

Anne and her sister died of typhus in March 1945 at Bergen Belsen. Otto Frank survived the war and on his return to Amsterdam he found that his daughter's diary was still intact.

Given to Anne for her thirteenth birthday, it provides a fascinating commentary on human courage and frailty and an articulate self-portrait of a sensitive and spirited young woman whose life was cut tragically short. The book is a powerful reminder of the horrors of war and an eloquent testament to the tenacity of the human spirit.

9. BOOTS BOOKLOVERS HOVER ON THE BRINK OF A NEW AND HOSTILE WORLD

"My friend and I have belonged to Boots' library for years and as perhaps you know they are very soon to close all their branches. This is going to be an awful blow to us all - especially as we live in a rather out of the way place and we wonder if there is anything you can do to make them change their minds?"

Excerpt from a letter sent to Mills and Boon. 1965.

Membership of Boots library soared to around the million mark during the Second World War, when 1,250,000 books were bought each year to supply 460 libraries. But storm clouds were gathering and an uncertain future loomed.

The post war years brought huge social and economic change. Public libraries were becoming more attractive and beginning to shake off their working class image. However, many of their Librarians were disinclined to spend time pandering to people whose literary diet consisted solely of light romances or westerns. They believed the library shelves should contain more edifying titles and this attitude prevented many Booklovers from discarding their Boots subscriptions.

But during the 1950s, public library policy changed and generous supplies of popular novels were purchased. This meant that readers with a flexible taste in fiction were better catered for. And Boots were finding it difficult to provide the costly services which had set them apart from public libraries and helped to attract more affluent members of society. Subscription rates had always been modest and in over sixty years, only slowly edged their way up to an annual thirty shillings.

There was consternation in well-heeled circles when Boots abandoned their On Demand service, which had guaranteed that any book ordered would be provided within three days.

This left only two types of subscription - the A class, which included access to recently published books and the B class, which included all but the very latest titles.

Boots assured its readers that new books which were specifically requested would be supplied as soon as possible but they were no longer prepared to make any promises about timescale. This upset those subscribers who were paying mainly for the privilege of reading new books hot off the press and it heralded the start of Boots downgrading the unique service it had provided.

Before the Second World War, an average lower middle class family would probably buy The Daily Express and maybe treat the kids to the Beano or the Dandy most weeks. Generally speaking, the British were not a book-buying nation but the arrival of the first cheap Penguin paperback changed that attitude forever. Books were no longer an expensive luxury and buying one's own pristine copy became a viable alternative to borrowing a well-thumbed one from the library.

Penguin books were first published in July 1935, with an initial ten titles. They were priced at just six pence each - a bargain compared to hardback books, which cost seven or eight shillings. The intention was to exercise a cultural influence but not be so highbrow as to alienate the general reader. The very first authors included Dorothy Sayers, Beverley Nichols and Compton Mackenzie, which suggests that Penguin did not have in their sights those readers addicted to light romances. However, anyone looking for a good read might well be tempted to buy the paperbacks and build up their own collection.

Penguins were a great success and by the middle of the 20th century the company was rivalling Boots Booklovers in its established position as a well-respected national institution. The circulating libraries were still forced to buy expensive hardback books because of their durability. Strapped for cash, they contemplated the possibility of saving money by rebinding paperbacks in hard covers. But Penguin, flexing its brash and youthful muscles, led a move within publishing to prevent this happening.

Boots libraries were struggling to survive in the modern post war world. Their main rival - Mudie's - had thrown in the towel as early as 1937, much to the horror of their clientele, who could hardly have been more shocked if the Bank of England had failed. But it was not until the 1950s and 60s that other commercial libraries gave up the fight.

The cheap twopenny libraries, which operated from corner shops and supplied only the lightest fiction at a cost of 2d a book, were unable to sustain even a meagre profit. This was echoed at the other end of the social scale, where independent libraries situated within the hallowed halls of Gentlemen's Clubs, also found themselves strapped for cash. An old Etonian, looking for a comfortable chair beside a welcoming fire, could no longer rely on a selection of favourite titles to enjoy, while he relaxed over a glass of old malt.

Boots libraries were caught up in a vortex of falling membership and rising costs. Older readers dominated the membership and newcomers were hard to find. Salaries and costs continued their relentless climb, while income from subscriptions plummeted. Putting prices up would be self-defeating, since membership would only decline further, while expenditure on books remained much the same. The purpose of Boots libraries had never been to make a huge profit but more to attract people into the stores. However, relentless losses on such a scale could not be tolerated.

W.H. Smith's succumbed first. In 1961, they closed all their libraries, having agreed with Boots that unexpired tickets could be used in their branches, if Smith's subscribers preferred not to take the option of a refund. After closure, it was revealed that the libraries had been losing up to £50,000 annually. The 750,000 books were either sold off in the bookshops or offered for sale to other libraries. None were transferred to Boots.

Unsurprisingly, this development fuelled conjecture about the Booklovers libraries. The Head Librarian, E.S. Moore, who had succeeded Freddie Richardson on his retirement in 1941, attempted to foil speculation that Boots libraries were in terminal decline. In a letter to the Times Literary Supplement on 15th December 1961, he wrote:

"Sir - on page 873 of your last issue, I read that there are rumours that Boots may close down their circulating libraries. May I say that I know of no foundation whatsoever for any such rumours. You are probably aware that we took over many of W.H. Smith's subscribers when they closed earlier this year."

But Boots certainly was considering the future of its libraries, even if it was unwilling to admit this publicly. Research revealed that the libraries did not make as big a contribution to the business as had been thought. Subscribers were mainly middle aged or elderly, accustomed to exceptional personal service and generally quite hard to please. They demanded high standards and expected to find a wide choice of books on the highly polished shelves.

A team of clerical staff at Boots' Head Office at Stamford Street in London, were assigned to come up with some solutions. Attempts were made to streamline clerical practices but Freddie Richardson had devised a series of complicated systems, which defied all but a total overhaul of procedures.

One of the major reasons for reaching a decision to close the libraries was the fact that space was needed for other merchandise. Boots was expanding its range of goods and needed to use the library areas more effectively.

On 28th April 1965, a press statement was issued, confirming the sad news.

"Boots announce with great regret that their Booklovers Library, which has provided a service for more than 65 years, will be coming to an end during the next twelve months."

The announcement paid tribute to the influence of Florence Boot, the first Lady Trent and to the loyalty of subscribers over the previous decades.

"We have always tried to maintain the standard of service they expect and deserve. It is significant, however, that the younger generation is not attracted to the idea of a circulating library. They turn either to the public libraries or buy paperbacks, where there has been a tremendous increase in sales. It would be quite wrong to conclude that people aren't reading as much as they did - everything indicates that they are. Yet the fact remains that they appear to prefer either to buy a book or borrow one locally from a public library."

The Company's comment about young people finding subscription libraries unappealing, demonstrates its recognition of a fast changing world. The genteel middleclass atmosphere of a Booklovers library would hold no allure for a youthful product of the Swinging Sixties.

Boots placed no blame on the advent of television, conceding that reading as a pastime was definitely not in decline. For an avid reader, the TV was no substitute for a book. But Boots libraries found themselves unable to attract new customers and by 1965 the number of subscribers had fallen from the peak of one million during the war to only 140,000.

1966 is remembered as being the year when England won the World Cup, the BBC introduced colour TV and 116 children and 28 adults died after a mountain of coal waste fell onto the village of Aberfan, in South Wales.

It was also the year in which the remaining handful of Boots libraries opened their doors to booklovers for the final time. On 5th February 1966, a depleted band of faithful and bewildered subscribers gathered around the shelves, buying a few remaining books and bidding farewell to staff.

Many distressed customers were indeed devastated by the closure of the library. It had provided them not only with books to read but friendly staff and a comfortable environment, in which to meet other Booklovers.

Mr Binney, who had been appointed Head Librarian in 1963 and who supervised the closure of the libraries, received many letters from inconsolable former subscribers. An article in the company magazine - "The Bee and the Beacon", contained the following account written by Miss Grace Bridge, who worked at branch 191, in Leicester.

"The last few weeks were sad ones for both librarians and subscribers. There were tears. And the almost unanswerable enquiries: "Where can we go now? What shall we do?" Our subscribers liked to talk and expected us to sympathise and advise on their trials and tribulations."

Miss Bridge believed that the library had been a valuable means of encouraging Boots trade.

*"We were told that the library was not a sales department. Perhaps not. But you know, we **did** sell. What of those slide boxes we sold for the holiday films? The Strepsils, Fenox and Tussils? The hand cream for those "spring cleaning" hands? Or the wedding presents we were asked to suggest? We nearly always made a sale, even though the money went in someone else's till. It was all part of our library service."*

Miss Bridge ended her account on a poignant note:

"Now the subscribers are gone, the book shelves bare and the department echoes the noise of shop fitters' tools."

Shelving was in fact frequently put to good use, as Boots book selling department often moved into the former library area. This did at least enable some appropriate use to be made of the well-appointed libraries. Like W.H. Smith's, Boots sold off as many books as possible and the surviving few were donated to hospitals and nursing homes.

As the months passed, it became obvious that readers of romantic fiction were the ones suffering most from the closure. Public libraries were still not buying enough of this genre to keep devotees adequately supplied.

Romantic fiction fans tended to be voracious readers, devouring three or four books a week. Public libraries often settled for second best and bought reprints, which both disappointed and failed to satisfy former Boots subscribers, who were accustomed to finding a selection of brand new romances on the shelves every week.

Since the 1920s, the publisher Mills & Boon had been a giant in the field of light fiction. They had unerringly identified their market, which was demonstrated by a well groomed middle class woman, pictured on the back of one of their books - declaring:

"I always look for a Mills & Boon when I want a pleasant book. Your troubles are at an end when you choose a Mills & Boon novel. No more doubts! No more disappointments! A Mills & Boon book will give you hours of happy reading."

Obviously these publishers were hard hit by Boots library closure, when they lost one of their main buyers. Some local authorities refused to purchase any Mills & Boon titles but most simply weren't prepared to give that genre a higher priority than any other. While some prejudice probably did enter into the decision making process, finally it all boiled down to making the public purse stretch as far as possible and trying to suit every type of reading taste.

John Boon, of Mills & Boon, became embroiled in the light fiction debate which took place in the mid sixties. He drew attention to the dilemma faced by "disinherited" readers:

"Dear Librarian. At the end of January, the last library belonging to Messrs Boots closed down and so in the space of twelve months, well over 100,000 subscribers have been compelled to look elsewhere for their books. Where are they to go? To cope with the influx of new members is a problem in itself for the public libraries, but, more difficult, some libraries still stock little or even no "entertainment reading" or "light fiction", therefore these people will be without the books they enjoy."

John Boon had received many forlorn and plaintive letters from readers deprived of their favourite genre. The following example illustrates their heart-rending plight:

"My friend and I have belonged to Boots' library for years and as perhaps you know they are very soon to close all their branches, this is going to be an awful blow to us all - especially as we live in a rather out of the way place and we wonder if there is anything you can do to make them change their minds or perhaps you have some other idea, we would all be so grateful for any help and suggestions you may be able to make."

Another letter showed the difficulty of obtaining Mills and Boon books in a public library:

"I have been receiving your lists of publications for some time but unfortunately I cannot make use of them in the future. As Boots' library has closed in Ashford I am now having to use the public library. When I asked for one of Essie Summer's books, I was told that it was not "in the scope of the library." I am writing to the chairman of the County Library Committee, Springfield, Maidstone, Kent, to ask for such books to be included."

Public libraries appear to have responded sympathetically to the issues raised in John Boon's letter, although they continued to plead lack of funding:

"The mailing produced a good humoured and interesting response. Many librarians replied that they bought Mills & Boon in varying numbers. Many spoke of limited funds at their disposal and stressed the need for reprints, i.e. something between the high priced first edition and the low priced paperback."

But despite good will on the part of public libraries, there remained a problematic void, created by the demise of Boots Booklovers Libraries. An article published in the

Bookseller in 1966, illustrates the plight of disinherited subscribers:

"I am one of that vast number of women who nowadays lead the dual life of the office-household variety, daily coping with many and varied problems and for me, books transform leisure into utmost pleasure.

I live in a large, northern industrial city with a population of approximately 265,000 and until a few months ago like many other women, and a fair sprinkling of men, spent very pleasant times in our local Boots Library, chatting about and choosing books.

Oh, the moans and groans when we were told that the library was closing! For we all knew the prospects before us were bleak, only three lending libraries now remaining in the city centre, two of which (the public library and a Literary Society) although extremely good, are limited in scope so far as concerns light fiction.

The third is a small fiction library run by a department store, lending books at the rate of 6d per volume per week. It is very popular but most of the books are several years old and there is a lengthy waiting list for the latest publications."

This article confirms that a visit to Boots library was a social event, as well as a book borrowing one. It is also a reminder of the superb service provided by Boots, for over sixty years. True, affluent readers had to pay a high price for their "Guaranteed" subscriptions, which enabled them to receive new books on publication but they were richly rewarded by a steady and speedy flow of the latest titles.

Former Boots librarians who moved into the public sector, remember their aggrieved subscribers attempting to challenge the County Council policy on the purchase of fiction. However, change only happened slowly and it wasn't until the late 70s and early 80s, that light romance was permitted more shelf space. The public libraries bore no similarity to Boots. The scale of operation, administrative demands and career ladder, produced a very different environment.

Harrods and a few of the twopenny libraries were now the only remaining places where people paid to borrow books. Soon, the mighty Harrods had this market all to itself and somehow managed to shepherd its subscription library safely through the turbulent post-war years. The library was situated on the fourth floor of the store and there were twelve desks, each staffed by one senior and two junior librarians, who scurried into work via a tunnel, on the other side of the road from the main shoppers entrance.

Harrods' prosperous subscribers did not even need to leave home. They could order a book over the telephone in the morning and it would be delivered later that same day, sometimes by horse-drawn van. Harrods library kept going until 1989, the same year that it introduced a dress code policy. Although not so strictly adhered to nowadays, shoppers wearing cycling shorts or swimming trunks may still be refused entry.

The closure of Boots and W.H Smith's circulating libraries in the 1960's had a lasting influence on the light fiction market, which slid into something of a decline. The desire for love stories remained but many adherents rebelled against actually buying those books for which they yearned, still hankering after borrowing them from the libraries.

But it wasn't only these readers who were making more demands on the public purse. Former subscribers wishing to read the latest best-selling novel or biography were to be found queuing at the library counter first thing every Monday morning, with a list of titles compiled from the review columns of the Sunday papers. The lists of reservations for popular new books soared, forcing the purchase of multiple copies and instigating querulous mutters from harassed staff, along the lines of: "This isn't Boots, you know."

The hey-day of the Boots Booklovers Library was the 1930s and 1940s and even then, recouping costs relied very much on a flourishing trade in the sale of second hand books. The "Guaranteed" subscription, which entitled the reader to receive new books on publication, was a very expensive service and bore no relation to the price of the subscription. With the arrival of hard times, it was inevitable that the "Guaranteed" service would have to come to an end.

Given the many factors working against them, it is probably surprising that Boots libraries survived for as long as they did. The loyalty of its remaining subscribers was evident and keeping so many branches open until 1966, was in some ways an act of goodwill towards this steadfast little nucleus of faithful customers.

Jesse Boot and his long serving Head Librarian, Freddie Richardson achieved their goal of making the libraries a positive advert for the Company brand and, without a doubt, they made a significant contribution to its reputation for service and quality.

Gone but not quite forgotten. Former subscribers and members of staff retain affectionate memories of Boots Booklovers Library, which was immortalised in John Betjeman's "Westminster Abbey."

> *"Think of What Our Nation Stands For,*
>
> *Books from Boots and Country Lanes,*
>
> *Free Speech, Free Passes, Class Distinction,*
>
> *Democracy and Proper Drains."*

Sources

I sent letters to forty regional newspapers, asking former Boots library staff and subscribers to contact me and in reply I received dozens of emails, letters and phone calls. Everyone who responded had memories and anecdotes.

For research purposes I read, consulted and used the following:

A Master's Dissertation by Rachel E. Theobald on "Boots Booklovers Library 1899 - 1966".

Photocopies from the Boots archive of:

"Books in Circulation in Boots Booklovers Library - 1919."

"A Record of New and Popular Books lately added to the Library - 1939"

Notes on examination papers set for library staff in the late 1940s.

A complete set of the Revised Instruction Circular Letters (The Rule Book) which was sent to every library, with regular updates. The set I used was dated 1932.

"Florence Boot: 1863-1952". A 7000 word article provided for research by Boots archive.

John Betjeman's poem "In Westminster Abbey" *Think of What Our Nation Stands For, Books from Boots and Country Lanes.*

Dorothy Whipple "The Priory" (1939) and "They Were Sisters" (1943)

E.M. Delafield "Diary of a Provincial Lady" (1930)

Nicola Beauman "A Very Great Profession" (1983)

Nickianne Moody   "Gendering Library History" (2001) Particularly the essay entitled: "Fashionable Design & Good Service: the Spinster Librarians at Boots Booklovers Library"

Judith Wright.   Boots Archivist.   "A History of Boots Booklovers' Library".   Article in Library and Information History Group Newsletter.   Dated Winter 2011.

I would like add here how grateful I am to Judith for all the help she gave me with my research.

Nicola Humble "The Feminine Middlebrow Novel: 1920s to 1950s" (2001)

James G Olle "The Lost Libraries".   Article in the Library Review, dated Autumn 1966.

Christine Poulson "Hidden Treasures". Article published in "The Author" Winter 2006.

"Boots, Stock and Branch".   Article published in the TLS, dated February 3rd 1966.

PRESS STATEMENT: "Closing of Boots Booklovers Library." Dated 28th April 1965.

Ruth Sears.   "BBL: 1899 to 1966".   Article in the Nottinghamshire Historian. 2008.

Christopher Weir "Jesse Boot Of Nottingham".   Published by Boots in 1994.

J.E. Greenwood "A Cap for Boots."   Published by Ebury Press. 1977.

Stephanie Spencer "Gender, work and education in Britain in the 1950s."

Palgrave Macmillan. 2005.

About the Author

Jackie Winter worked for 22 years in Dorset County Libraries. A colleague and friend had previously been a Boots library assistant and clearly very much enjoyed the work.

Jackie became intrigued by the many differences between public and subscription libraries. She began writing articles about BBL but the research was so fascinating that a book became the inevitable result.

Had Jackie belonged to Boots library she would undoubtedly have been a Class B subscriber, resentfully envious of the elite Class A folk who had first pick of all the new books.

Jackie is an avid reader and a loyal member of Wimborne Library. One of her favourite writers is Dorothy Whipple, most of whose books were published in the interwar years and would have been enjoyed by many a Boots Booklover.

Also by Jackie Winter

Life in Tandem – Tales of Cycling Travels (Chantries Press 2013)

Praise for Jackie Winter's Life in Tandem

"Her narrative flows as smoothly as a gear change on a well-oiled 10 speed derailleur."

"The next page beckons and the last page arrived too soon – rather like a good cycle tour."

"One of those books that you do not want to end."

"The author's dry wit and excellent narrative style always shines through."

22267321R00081

Printed in Great Britain
by Amazon

JEREMY BROWN:SPY

THREE BOOKS IN ONE!

ORIGINALLY PUBLISHED IN 3 SEPARATE VOLUMES
JEREMY BROWN OF THE SECRET SERVICE
JEREMY BROWN AND THE MUMMY'S CURSE
JEREMY BROWN ON MARS

First published in three volumes by
Walker Books Ltd. 1997, 1998

This edition published in the
United Kingdom in 2010
by Simon Cheshire
www.simoncheshire.co.uk

A CIP catalogue record of this book is available
from the British Library

ISBN 978-0-9565049-0-6

Cover illustration by George & Isobel Cheshire

aBOUT THe aUTHOR

Simon Cheshire is the author of many hugely popular
books for children and teenagers, including the
bestselling Saxby Smart detective stories. He writes in
a tiny little office, which used to be a cupboard, and
which is bursting at the seams with books, old
chocolate wrappers and letters from his readers. He
writes using an Apple Mac and a mug of coffee. Many
of his best ideas come to him while he's staring out of
the window. He lives in Warwick, but spends most of
his time in a world of his own.

Also available

They Melted His Brain!
Totally Unsuitable For Children
Bottomby

Saxby Smart: Private Detective series
The Curse of the Ancient Mask
The Fangs of the Dragon
The Pirate's Blood
The Hangman's Lair
The Eye Of The Serpent
Five Seconds To Doomsday
The Poisoned Arrow
Secret Of The Skull

SImON CHeSHIRe
WWW.SIMONCHESHIRE.CO.UK

JEREMY BROWN OF
THE SECRET SERVICE

CHAPTER ONE

In which Jeremy Brown nearly gets duffed up

Jeremy Brown had a secret. His parents didn't know what it was, his sisters didn't know what it was, and neither did his teachers. Patsy Spudd, his best friend at school, she knew all about it, but she was sworn to secrecy.

However, things will get pretty confusing if his secret isn't revealed, so: Jeremy Brown was an MI7 agent. His boss at MI7 reckoned Jeremy was pretty excellent when it came to foiling evil plots of international proportions. And so did Jeremy. Mind you, his missions were never accomplished easily. For example:

It was a Tuesday, and the weather was grumpy. Jeremy Brown on his way to school, swinging his bag and watching the clouds grumbling around the sky. He was quite short, quite scruffy, and quite unable to see properly without his glasses. He didn't notice Sharkface until he walked right slap-bang into him. Jeremy bounced back and landed with a thud on the pavement. Sharkface didn't. Sharkface stayed exactly where he was.

His name wasn't really Sharkface of course. His name was Mark, but Mark rhymed with shark, and his strange, long nose made his head look sort of wedge-shaped. Even then, people might not have called him Sharkface had it not been for the fact that he was the nastiest bully in the school.

Jeremy couldn't run away, because Sharkface would chase him and duff him up. He couldn't stay where he was, because then Sharkface would simply duff him up right here. Either way, he was going to get his blazer torn. The situation looked hopeless. (It wasn't really hopeless, as you can guess from the title of this chapter, but Jeremy felt hopeless anyway.)

"Brown," said Sharkface, nastily.

Jeremy felt like saying "What a wonderful memory for names you have, Sharkface," but he didn't. It would only have made Sharkface angry. So instead, he made a sort of wimpering noise. This was more in line with what Sharkface expected.

"I don't like you, Brown. You're a little weed with specs," he said, even more nastily.

"I-I just want to get to school," said Jeremy, as bravely as the situation would allow. Not very bravely at all, to be honest.

"I got an idea," said Sharkface, in the nastiest way possible. If he'd been a cartoon character, a light bulb would have appeared in a puff of smoke above his head. "I'm going to turn you upside down and bounce you on your head." He smiled. It looked horrible.

He reached down with both his thick, meaty fists, and lifted Jeremy off his feet. Jeremy could smell salt and vinegar crisps on Sharkface's breath. He felt something go tight in his stomach.

He braced himself and gritted his teeth.

Suddenly, there was a flash of ginger hair, and the swoosh of a school bag being swung through the air. The bag whopped Sharkface in the teeth, and he dropped Jeremy, who found himself back on the pavement staring at the sky.

"Oh no, it's Patsy Spudd!" moaned Sharkface.

"What a wonderful memory for names you have, Sharkface," said Patsy.

That made Sharkface angry. He leaped at Patsy with a rumbling grunt. Patsy dodged quickly, and he toppled into a tangle of tree-trunk arms and legs in the gutter.

Patsy stood over him, with her freckle-dotted nose in the air. Or, rather, she stood next to him, since he was at least twice her height, even when he was in a tangle of arms and legs in the gutter.

"Pick on someone you own size," said Patsy, loftily. "Come on, Jeremy." She pulled him to his feet and they ran. Sharkface watched them for a moment, with his mouth wriggling into a sneer. It was his way of trying to look tough when he knew perfectly well that he looked silly.

As soon as they were out of his sight, Patsy gave Jeremy a kick on the shin. "Ow!" yelped Jeremy. "What was that for?"

"Relying on me to rescue you," said Patsy grumpily.

"I keep telling you, I can't blow my cover," whispered Jeremy. "Brilliantly clever and highly trained agents like me must stay in the shadows. I have to pretend to be Sharkface-food at all times."

"Don't I know it," muttered Patsy.

An hour later, they were at Grotside School, room H4, in the middle of Mr Tudor's History class.

Meanwhile, in his office, the Headmaster of Grotside School was carefully folding an origami elephant. The Headmaster was very round, with a red face and sausage-y fingers, but he folded his paper models with great delicacy and skill. The little finger on each hand pointed outwards as he completed the creature's trunk.

The *BBBBrrrr-TTttrrrr* of the phone made him jump. He twirled in his enormous chair, and the last whisps of grey hair that clung to his head twirled with him.

"Yes! Headmaster!" he barked.

"No, you're the Headmaster," said the voice on the phone.

The Headmaster sat up suddenly, and his origami elephant spun to the floor. He'd heard this voice before. His face went a purply shade of mauve.

"Now listen here!" he snapped. "I don't know who you are, but you're not getting me to let Brown and Spudd off school again!"

"Then I presume," said the voice softly, "that you don't mind if the whole world finds out you wear underpants with Frank The Cuddly Bunny on them?"

A purply shade of mauve was no longer good enough. The Headmaster went white. "H-H-How..? How did you..? I'll have their letters of authorisation ready in ten minutes."

To find out whose voice that was, Jeremy and Patsy's history lesson will have to be interrupted. This won't bother either of them one little bit.

Just as Mr Tudor was describing the arrival of the Spanish Armada, Jeremy's left thumb began to tingle. Either he'd accidentally bashed it with a hammer (not very likely in the middle of History), or he was about to get an important message.

"Sir!" he yelled. "Sir! Got to go to the toilet!"

The rest of the class giggled. All except Patsy, who realised what was up.

"Can't it wait, Brown?" said Mr Tudor.

"No, sir! Bursting!" Jeremy jigged about a bit in his chair for added effect. Mr Tudor waved a weary hand and Jeremy dashed from the room.

Out in the corridor, he activated

the communicator hidden under his left thumbnail. It was a silly place to have hidden it, because pulling the miniature aerial out always hurt.

"Ooo, ow!"

The earpiece was concealed under his right thumbnail. He spoke into his left thumb, with his right thumb jabbed into his ear. He put on a very serious expression and gave his identification code: "MI7, the custard is banana flavoured."

"With fruit portions," said the voice. "Pay attention. This is Control. Three hours ago, the Com-Star communications satellite developed a fault and dropped out of orbit. It will crash somewhere in your sector in approximately fifteen minutes. It's designed to withstand impact, so it should land in one piece. It's roughly the size and shape of a dustbin. Your mission is to retrieve it, before anyone else does."

"Anyone else?" muttered Jeremy, slightly worried.

"It contains experimental computers which are years ahead of their time, stuff that any of the world's worst villains would pay millions for."

The bell rang, doors opened, and the corridor was suddenly filled with the sounds of clattering feet and chattering voices. Patsy appeared as Jeremy quickly pushed the miniature aerial back into place. "Ooo, ow!"

"Are we off?" said Patsy, excitedly.

"We're off," said Jeremy. And off they went.

As they left the building, the Headmaster came running up to them, puffing and panting, his arms flapping. He handed them each a letter of permission to be out of school. He had a helpless grin on his face, and kept dabbing a hanky to his forehead.

"Here you are," he said with a trembling voice. "Err, have a nice time." He scurried back to his office, as fast as he could.

They hurried to the school gates, and Jeremy told Patsy about the message from HQ. "How can they be sure it's going to fall somewhere around here?" said Patsy.

"Well, err, they'll have followed it's trajectory... thingummy. Or something," said Jeremy, who should have paid more attention during Maths.

It was time to set off on another mission which was daring, dangerous, deadly and maybe one or two other things beginning with 'd'. It was also time for Jeremy to smarten himself up. His scruffiness was just a disguise. He stood up straight, tied his shoelaces, and popped his glasses into his top pocket. He pulled up his tie and made his eyes go all narrow and tough-looking. "Yeh, all narrow and tough-looking. Proper spy look," he muttered to himself.

Patsy, on the other hand, was quite happy to be her normal self: ketchup-stained and looking like she'd been dragged through a hedge backwards. "Come on," she said. "We haven't got long."

CHAPTER TWO
**In which an evil scheme is hatched,
and a satellite drops to Earth.**

Meanwhile, on the other side of town, in an abandoned factory, deep in the remains of a damp and musty basement, three of the country's most notorious and evil villains were practising their French.

"Vooz ett ern... cosh-on trez gross," said the first one, whose name was Kenneth. He was approximately eight feet tall, with shoulders like two medium-sized sheep fighting under a blanket, and a face like a bulldog chewing a scorpion. As he read the words, he followed them on the page with a grubby thumb. "You are a very fat pig."

"Vooz ett ern cosh-on trez gross," repeated his younger brother, who looked exactly the same, and who was also called Kenneth. Their mother had been a terribly confused woman.

They were reading an article entitled "How To Insult People In 13 Languages," which appeared in the new issue of *Thug!* the club magazine of ROTTEN (the Rancid Organisation for Terror, Threats, Evil and Nastiness).

The third villain, a tall and wiry man with a tall and wiry moustache, stepped out of the shadows. His name was Sid Lime, and his eyes appeared to have been borrowed from one of those paintings which follow you around the room in creepy old houses. "Amateurs," he spat with a growl.

"We're expund— expind— we're biggering our education," said Kenneth and Kenneth together. First-Kenneth scratched his head, and Second-Kenneth scratched his bottom.

"Listen," hissed Sid quietly. He didn't need to hiss quietly, because there was nobody for miles around to overhear him. He reckoned it was a more villainous thing to do, so he hissed quietly anyway. "Listen, you micro-brained dollops of chimp poo. While you've been eating extra bananas to get enough skins to slip under the feet of old ladies, some of us have been doing serious research."

With a flourish of paper, he flicked open his copy of *Wrong Doer* the newsletter of SCUM (the Society of Criminals - the U and the M didn't stand for anything, but SC didn't sound like much on its own). "There! Read the headline!"

First-Kenneth mouthed the words carefully. "I Lied, Confesses Frankenstein - Monster Was Man In Suit!"

"No, above that," said Sid.

"Five Minutes To Go Until Satellite Hits Town - Dash For Computer Secrets Is On!"

Sid folded the newspaper with a couple of lightning movements and stuffed it in his pocket. "By the end of the day, gentlemen, we will be richer than a millionaire in a thick chocolate sauce. Move out!"

Sid marched towards the stairs, cackling in the high-pitched manner approved by the official SCUM handbook. Kenneth and Kenneth followed, giggling excitedly.

Sid's voice echoed around the dripping, shadowy walls. "Hurry, gentlemen, I estimate that the satellite will appear in the sky any second now!"

"Patsy, I estimate that the satellite will appear in the sky any second now," said Jeremy, peering through his binoculars and tapping his pocket calculator. They were standing on the corner of the high street, getting funny looks from shoppers.

"Whereabouts?" said Patsy, looking up and leaning back as far as she dared.

"Umm, up there somewhere, definitely." He tapped at his pocket calculator a bit more.

"I'd guess," said Patsy thoughtfully, "that it'll appear as a small red streak of flame, visible on a direct line from this spot past the roof of the supermarket."

Jeremy stopped tapping and looked at her, eyes wide. "That's a very precise and confident prediction," he said, flicking a bit of fluff off his sleeve. "How can you know that?"

"Because there's a small red streak of flame visible on a direct line from this spot past the roof of the supermarket."

Jeremy whirled around and looked at the red streak through his binoculars for a moment. "Now, judging from the angle of decent *(-tap -tap -tap -tap)* and the speed of motion *(-tap -tap -tap -tap)*, and all that kind of stuff, we can calculate that it will land in *(-tap)*, crumbs, Brazil!"

Patsy snatched the calculator from him. "Oh, give it here." She did her own sums. "It's coming down somewhere near the sewage works," she mumbled.

"Oh YUK!" cried Jeremy. "I'll get FILTHY!"

Patsy consulted her fold-out map of the town. "Ah, no, not the sewage works..."

"Thank goodness for that," sighed Jeremy.

"It's going to land on the school."

"WHAT?!" cried Jeremy.

"Exactly!" cried Patsy, flipping her hair out of her eyes. "The school will have to be evacuated!"

"No," said Jeremy, "I mean, 'What? We've got to go all the way back there again?' It's miles. Did I ever tell you about the time I was blasted 476 kilometres into space by a pair of exploding socks?"

"Many times," said Patsy wearily.

They set off for the school. Jeremy hoped that, whatever happened, they didn't come face to face with a gang of desperate, greedy criminals.

Meanwhile, the gang of desperate, greedy criminals had got a head start on them. Sid, Kenneth and Kenneth were sitting outside the school gates in Sid's huge, black car. Sid was keeping a beady eye out for trouble. Kenneth and

Kenneth just had beady eyes.

Sid glanced up at the sky and caught sight of the red streak. Then he glanced at the school gates and caught sight of Jeremy and Patsy hurrying towards the main buildings. His brain put two and two together, made three, and added one. "They know what's going to happen," he hissed quietly (hissing quietly was probably the right thing to do this time, since our heroes might possibly have overheard him). "They must be working for the cops, or MI7, or something else disgustingly well-behaved."

The red streak was getting brighter now, and larger every second. Jeremy and Patsy could hear a high-pitched whine, getting steadily louder.

"What do we do about them, boss?" said First-Kenneth.

("Bet he says to get 'em," whispered Second-Kenneth).

"Do, gentlemen? We GET THEM!" shouted Sid. ("Told yer," said Second-Kenneth with a grin, clapping his hands in glee).

Sid slammed his foot down on the accelerator, and the car's wheels squealed as they spun into action. The car leaped forwards, heading straight for Jeremy and Patsy.

The car bounded past the gates at top speed. Its engine roared.

Jeremy was looking the other way. "That satellite sounds ever so near," he said.

Patsy spun on her heels. The car was almost upon them! No place to run! She leapt sideways, knocking Jeremy off his feet. The two of them dived out of the way as the car screeched past them. The tires missed their feet by millimetres. Sid hissed with anger.

"Of all the rotten luck," said Jeremy, dusting grass off his trousers. "A gang of desperate, greedy criminals."

"Are we going back to get them again?" said Second-Kenneth.

"No, pea-head, we're going to get to that satellite before they do!" spat Sid. The car shot on towards the school buildings. All that blocked their way was Sharkface.

By now, the red streak in the sky had become a flaming column of smoke. It whistled as it plummeted through the air, closer, closer.

Suddenly, the satellite came screaming out of the clouds, and whalloped smack through the roof of the school with a sound which can't really be put into a word but which was more or less *WHHHhhhAAAA-aaammmmM!!* A explosion of dust, debris and sections of roof puffed out into the sky.

"Quick!" yelled Jeremy, standing at a slight angle to look all heroic. "Those villains mustn't get to it first."

Patsy's hands were pressed to the side of her head. Luckily, what she said next turned out to be completely untrue, so there's no need to worry: "I bet it's gone through about three floors. I bet there are loads of injuries and blood all over the place."

Sharkface stood in the way of Sid's

car, hands on hips, sneer on face. He wasn't being brave, just plain stupid. Sid put his foot down. Sharkface tried to jump, too late. Next thing he knew, he was clinging to the car's bonnet, one hand on each headlight. The car smashed through the doors of the main school building, scattering splinters of wood and terrified teachers.

"*Aaaarrrggghhhh!*" screamed Sharkface.

The sound of the car was deafening in the corridor. Its wheels spun, and it lurched forwards, then turned a sharp left and bump-bump-bumped up the stairs.

"That satellite's up here, and I want it!" said Sid.

"*Aaaarrrggghhhh!*" screamed Sharkface.

Back in the corridor, Jeremy flapped his arms to clear the smoke. Patsy picked up a chunk of door, ready for a fight.

"There's no need for that," said Jeremy. "All we need is a brilliant idea to get us up a couple of floors before their car can smash it's way there."

"Such as..?" said Patsy.

"The Chemistry lab!" cried Jeremy.

"But we're both terrible at Chemistry," said Patsy. "Everything we touch explodes."

"Exactly," said Jeremy. He dragged a desk out of the lab, into the corridor, and put another desk on top of it. Then he collected a large beaker and an armful of dangerous-looking substances. "Get in between the desks," he said. He mixed all the chemicals in the beaker, dropped it underneath the desks and jumped in beside Patsy.

With an almighty *WHUMPH*! the mixture ignited. It was a result which would have scored Jeremy zero in an exam, but which shot the desks, one secret agent and one secret agent's best friend through the ceiling, through another ceiling, and landed them in the Headmaster's office.

"Easy," coughed Jeremy through a cloud of dust. "Am I a genius or what?"

Meanwhile, the car revved up another flight of stairs. Sid spun the steering wheel, and the car ploughed through a bookcase. Mr Tudor jumped out of a hole in the wall to avoid the car, and dropped into the school swimming pool. As he fell, he thought sadly that maybe he wouldn't be able to spend nice a quiet afternoon marking homework after all.

First-Kenneth pointed a stubby finger at Sharkface, who was still clutching onto the bonnet of the car. "Hey, his head looks like a shark."

The car took the corner off a classroom, and a shower of plaster and falling bricks jerked it to a halt. Sharkface flew off the bonnet, flew out through an open window and joined Mr Tudor in the pool.

Sid, Kenneth and Kenneth climbed out of the vehicle. "Spread out, boys," said Sid, coughing as the dust settled. "It's around here somewhere."

And so it was. Nearby, in the

Headmaster's office, Jeremy and Patsy suddenly realised where they were, and prepared their apologies. Then they saw a large, scorched, cylindrical object, steaming gently and sitting in the spot usually occupied by the Headmaster. The Headmaster was under it, pinned to the floor. Origami animals were scattered all over the place. Luckily for the rest of the school, his stomach had broken the satellite's fall. He groaned painfully.

Jeremy and Patsy peeped over the edge of his desk and waved tiny little waves at him. They had sheepish smiles on their faces. "Hi, Sir," said Patsy. "Give us a minute, and we'll have this out of your way."

The Headmaster's face went the red it usually reserved for major breaches of school discipline, or parents' evenings. "Kfluff mnnemm flumm ploo!" he spluttered.

"He's reeeeally cross," said Patsy, fearfully. "Look, he's frothing at the mouth."

"No, I think he's just swallowed half a dozen origami animals," said Jeremy.

"Or perhaps," said a sinister voice behind them, "he's realised that the game is up."

Jeremy and Patsy spun around.

Several things could have happened at that point. The best thing would have been for Jeremy to secretly pick up a handful of plaster dust, fling it at the villains, escape with the satellite while the villains were yelping and rubbing their eyes, and have the three of them picked up by the police.

Unfortunately, all Jeremy could secretly pick up was a giraffe made out of a page of exercise book. He flung it anyway. It bounced off Second-Kenneth's nose.

"Oh rabbits," said Patsy. "I suppose this means we're going to be captured and locked up in a dark, stinking basement in the middle of nowhere."

CHAPTER THREE

In which our heroes are locked up in a dark, stinking basement in the middle of nowhere.

"You just had to say it, didn't you?" grumbled Jeremy. Patsy poked her tongue out at him.

The basement was even damper and mustier than it had been in Chapter Two. Grey-green mould grew in hideous lumps across one wall. The smell of week-old cabbage oozed through the air. A bottle of Super-Strong-Ultra-Germkill Detergent would have taken one look at the grime on the floor tiles and had a screaming fit. The only light came from a tiny, grimy window, way up high above them.

Jeremy and Patsy were sitting (carefully) on an upturned crate. Their left legs were chained to one of the many pipes which snaked around the walls.

Jeremy wriggled, a sour expression on his face. "I'm getting my best trousers all grubby now," he grumbled again. "And we've missed lunch."

Patsy was about to say "Stop thinking of your stomach for once and start thinking up brilliant ideas for getting us out of this dangerous and terrifying situation!" but was interrupted by the sound of the news on the little TV Kenneth and Kenneth were watching in the far corner. They weren't really interested in the news, they were waiting for the cartoons to come on.

"—which fell to Earth earlier today, landing safely on the stomach of a headmaster," said the tinny voice from the TV. "The disturbance at the school which followed was witnessed by teacher Brian Tudor."

"Brian," sniggered Patsy quietly.

Mr Tudor appeared on the screen, dabbing his face with a towel. "There were dozens of them," he said, trembling. "They drove through school in eight bulldozers! I blocked their way as best I could, but after a long fight I was hurled through the roof. Savages, that's what they were! Maniacs!"

The newsreader came back on screen. "By the time the police had sorted out what was going on here, then, the criminals and the satellite were long gone—"

Sid stabbed the OFF button. For a moment, the only sound was the dripping of a particularly nasty and germ-filled goo from the high ceiling. Then came the slow K-clack... K-clack... of Sid's boots as he walked slowly over to his prisoners. Behind him, Kenneth and Kenneth quietly set the TV to record the cartoons.

Jeremy, being a highly trained secret agent, faced Sid with a bold expression on his face, his back straight, his mouth set in a slight smile, a-ha, do your worst, vile villain.

Patsy, not being a secret agent, let her bottom lip wobble all over the place and looked terrified.

K-clack... K-clack... K-clack...

Sid had been on the phone for the past hour. He'd worked his way through the *Villains (International)* section of Yellow Pages, and had found the phone number of The World's Sneakiest High-Tech Bad Guy. The bad guy had been on the loo when Sid phoned, but his mum had got him to call back, and they'd settled on a price for the satellite. After he'd put the phone down, Sid had consulted his SCUM handbook, which had informed him that he should now approach his prisoners slowly, wearing noisy footwear in a threatening manner and say:

"Allow me to introduce myself. I am Sid Lime." The low, sinister sound of his voice bounced off the walls, found it had picked up something nasty from them, and died away.

"Good afternoon," said Jeremy politely. "I am Jeremy Brown of the Secret Service, and this is my sidekick Patsy." Patsy kicked his side. "Sorry, this is my Executive Assistant, Patsy."

Sid gave a high pitched cackle, as

recommended in the SCUM handbook. "Secret Service? Hah! Do they seriously believe that mere kiddies are going to stop me? I've just been on the phone to The World's Sneakiest High-Tech Bad Guy, and very soon I and my colleagues here are going to be so rich they'll have to invent a new word for greedy." He gave an even higher pitched cackle.

"They'll certainly have to invent a new word for ugly," said Jeremy.

Kenneth and Kenneth giggled, then realised he was talking about them too, and shut up. Sid leaned close to Jeremy, his yellowy teeth showing through a broad grin. This time, Jeremy could smell cheese and onion crisps.

"My colleagues and I are now off to the meeting point. By the time anyone finds you... IF anyone finds you, that is... we'll be thousands of miles away. Come, gentlemen, we have an appointment in three hours' time."

"Fatlywobblecash," said First-Kenneth.

"That could be a new word for

greedy," said Second-Kenneth.

"Shut up," said Sid. "Fetch the satellite and meet me by what's left of the car."

He ushered them out, pausing only to give Jeremy and Patsy a cheery wave. If his cackle had been any higher, it would have missed his face completely. The door slammed and locked behind him with a heavy CLAAANNG.

There was only the dripping of ooze from the ceiling.

"Oh dear," said Jeremy quietly.

Patsy kicked her leg about, making the chain rattle wildly. "Jeremy, old pal, now would be a good time to tell me that you've got a special chain-cutting type device hidden in your shoe, or a laser gun in a biro or something."

Jeremy raised an eyebrow. "Let's not be silly, Patsy."

"Can't you get MI7 on your radio?"

"We're in a basement, remember?" said Jeremy with a sigh. "That window way up there is at ground level. The signal won't reach them."

Patsy rattled her chain again, angrily. Rattling it made her feel better, so she rattled it some more. Meanwhile, Jeremy paced up and down as far as his own chain would take him. Wrapping a hanky around his hand to avoid contamination, he tapped gently at the pipework to which the other ends of their chains were attached.

"I wonder what's in these pipes?" he said, almost to himself. "If it's gas, or oil, we'd be in real trouble. Again. But if it's water…"

Patsy's freckled nose wrinkled excitedly. She could smell an escape plan taking shape, and escape plans usually meant a certain amount of noise, violence and damage to property. "What do you want me to break, JB?" she said, pulling up her socks and wiping her nose.

"These pipes," said Jeremy. "We'll both get wet, of course, but that's unavoidable. If the pipes carry water."

Patsy's leg swung back, ready to give the pipe an almighty whack. "And if it's oil?"

"We'll come to a sticky end."

"And if it's gas?"

"We'll get blown to bits."

Patsy stuck out her bottom lip and nodded thoughtfully. "Right, better give it a really good boot, then."

She kicked the pipe. It wobbled and clanked against the wall. Another kick. It bent with a screech of metal. Another. The bend became a dent. Another. The dent became a buckle. Another. The pipe cracked and snapped in two. The chains spun free.

Jeremy and Patsy's relief that it WAS water which shot out was quickly overcome by the fact that the water was absolutely freezing. As it hit them, they let out howls which would have got a werewolf through to the national finals of the All England Howling Championships. The water gushed and rushed across the basement floor, soaking everything.

"Ha-haaaa! Who's for a swim?" yelled Patsy, a broad grin across her face. Jeremy's teeth were chattering together to much for him to answer.

It took quite a while for the whole basement to fill with water, so we'll skip ahead, to the bit where they've floated up to the level of the window:

Water flowed all around them as they rose closer and closer to the ceiling. The broken pipe was way below them now, gushing silently in the murky depths of the room.

Patsy swam over to the window with a powerful front crawl. She grabbed the window frame with both hands.

"You'll have to give it a good pull, I expect," spluttered Jeremy, trying hard to keep afloat. Underwater, his arms and legs were doing a rapid doggy paddle. "Judging from the terrible pong in this room, that window hasn't been opened for years."

Patsy summoned up all her strength, then summoned up a double side order of extra strength just to make sure. The water rose higher, splashing the grime-streaked pane of glass. She breathed deeply, and gripped tighter. She pulled.

Nothing.

She pushed. Nothing.

"It won't budge!" she shrieked.

The water continued to rise. There was just enough room between it and the ceiling for their heads and shoulders now.

"Try again!" called Jeremy. "The window frame's bound to be rotten through."

She gripped hard and pulled, her face stretched tight with effort. Nothing. "Nothing!" she yelped.

The water rose up, and up. It was at the level of their chins. Patsy looked at Jeremy, and Jeremy looked at the window. So much for his escape plan.

"Hang on a mo," he said suddenly. He tried to doggie-paddle over to the window, but the strength of the water currents pulled him back into the centre of the room. He tried to shout to Patsy, but kept bobbing under the surface. All he could do was make a twisting motion with one hand.

"Huh?" said Patsy, frowning. She was having trouble keeping afloat herself. The water was close to the ceiling. The thick muck on the ceiling was making the water wish it had never left the pipe in the first place.

Suddenly, Patsy realised what Jeremy meant. She felt along the window frame, found a tiny little catch, and flipped it open.

Water gushed out into the open air, and the two of them gushed along with it.

They found themselves in a scruffy, weed-covered and now soaking wet courtyard. They staggered to their feet, coughing and trying to ignore the horrible smells that were clinging to their clothes. Patsy gave a thumbs-up sign. "That was fun!" she said, breathlessly.

Jeremy tried to smooth his hair back into place. "I really am quite frighteningly clever," he said. "Did I ever tell you about the time I escaped from a pit of poisonous snakes using only a rubber band, a silk handkerchief and a positive attitude?"

"Yes," said Patsy. "Call MI7, quick. The satellite could be anywhere by now."

Jeremy pulled out the hidden aerial of his communicator. "Ooo, oww!" He shook both thumbs a couple of times. "No good, it's completely waterlogged. We're on our own."

Patsy shook herself like a dog. "Oh rabbits. There must be some way of working out where they've gone. The ratty little one said they had a meeting in three hours. They also said they'd be thousands of miles away soon."

They stood and thought carefully for a moment.

CHAPTER FOUR

In which our heroes have worked out that the answer is the airport.

"Your attention please." A crisp, female voice echoed around the polished halls and corridors of the airport's Terminal One. "This is an important announcement. Will all passengers tronpolling on the glumpy plinky plonky, make sure that flumpy dinky doo, bim bom pilly clump. Thank you." (The airport announcer had done a special course in Sounding Like Gobbledegook. She'd come top of the class, ahead of several railway station announcers.)

Jeremy and Patsy had put on dark glasses in an effort to look more official and dangerous. Their clothes were crumpled and damp from the wet basement, so the effort was completely wasted. But they reckoned they looked pretty cool in shades, so they kept them on.

"We must try to blend in and be as inconspicuous as possible," whispered Jeremy. He straightened up his tie, which was now all twisted and curly, and they looked around at the shifting crowds of passengers and the blinking display screens.

"I can't see the blinking display screens 'cos of these blinking glasses," mumbled Patsy.

"Whassall this then?" said a low voice beside Jeremy's right ear. Jeremy almost jumped out of his skin. They turned to find a dozen security guards looming over them, with long riot sticks and short tempers at the ready.

"You are herewith looking of a highly suspicious and non-passenger style nature," said another guard.

"My name is Jeremy Brown," said Jeremy correctly, "and this is my... Operations Director, Patsy Spudd. Glad to see you guys are on the ball. We're on official business of a highly sensitive and non-airport style nature."

The guard with the narrowest eyes and the widest nose leaned closer. He sniffed at Jeremy, and his eyes suddenly widened in disgust. "If you're on official business, sonny Jim, then I'm the Queen of Sheba."

"We'd love to stay and chat, your majesty," said Jeremy, "but we've got important work to do catching a gang of international thieves."

Unfortunately, if there was one thing the security guards wouldn't stand for, it was someone else chasing villains in their airport. All together, they snatched pairs of handcuffs from their belts and flipped them open. "You're coming with us!" they all bellowed.

If there was one thing that Jeremy Brown was famed for at MI7, it was having amazing pieces of good luck at moments like this. The amazing piece of good luck he had at that moment involved a large crowd of Japanese tourists sweeping past, allowing him and Patsy to conceal themselves amongst luggage and souvenir hats. By the time the guards had stopped answering the tourists' questions about where to find the check-in desks and the toilets, Jeremy and Patsy had long gone. They sneaked away towards the Departure Lounge.

"Keep a lookout for a large rucksack," said Jeremy, "or something else large and travel-related that they might have stashed the satellite in. Even that lot aren't so stupid as to carry millions of pounds worth of stolen high technology on open view through a public place."

Meanwhile, First-Kenneth was dragging the satellite across the floor towards the airport's check-in desks. He was struggling because it weighed almost three tonnes, and because heat-scarred bits of it kept getting caught on the carpet. Second-Kenneth was too busy hitching his trousers up to help. It was Second-Kenneth's belt that his brother was using as a rope to pull the satellite with.

As he had been instructed by The World's Sneakiest High-Tech Bad Guy, Sid went to the third phone booth from the left, next to the queue for Flight DH103 to Spain. He dialled the number he'd been told to memorise. The World's Sneakiest High-Tech Bad Guy's mum let him know exactly where the plane would be waiting for them.

He returned to Kenneth and Kenneth.

"Gentlemen," he said quietly, his eyes darting in all directions to make sure nobody was sneaking up on them. "Everything is arranged."

"Can you see OK with your eyes doing that, boss?" said Second-Kenneth.

"Shut up. We now go to the Departure Lounge and wait for a contact to contact us. We will board the private jet of The World's Sneakiest High-Tech Bad Guy, we will be given a quite staggeringly large sum of money, and then his mum says it's OK to get a lift to South America. Oh, and we're to make sure he's wearing his woolly jumper. He's got all wet today, apparently, and he might have caught a chill."

They arrived at the Departure Lounge in the space of one short sentence. The satellite bumped along behind First-Kenneth, leaving a trail of little bits of metal behind it. Second-Kenneth scampered off to the shops to get some comics and sweeties for the journey. Sid found somewhere to sit away from the law-abiding folk.

Jeremy and Patsy, crawling along on their hands and knees to keep out of sight of the gang, were soon positioned underneath Sid's chair. (Alert readers will have already worked out how our heroes had tracked them down. Any readers who are not alert have missed out now.)

"Lucky you told them this gizmo was a shaving kit," dribbled Second-Kenneth to Sid, through a mouthful of licorice, "or we might not have got it through Customs."

"If we bring their buyer to justice,"

whispered Jeremy, "we could deal a deadly blow to world computer crime."

"Or at least give it a good poke in the eye," whispered Patsy.

"I'd be famous!" whispered Jeremy.

"No, I'd be famous. You're a secret agent."

"Oh yeh."

They didn't have long to wait. A figure walked briskly over to the gang. He was wearing a long, dark raincoat, black gloves and a wide-brimmed hat to keep his face in shadow. He looked every inch the scheming low-life. Sid was dead jealous.

"This way," he whispered. Jeremy only caught a brief glimpse of him, but thought there was something odd about the shape of his head.

Sid jumped to his feet. "Come along, gentlemen. Careful with the merchandise. Nice coat, by the way."

"Thanks," said the mysterious figure.

"Reeeeally dark."

"Thanks."

From their hiding place, Jeremy and Patsy saw four pairs of feet hurrying away, followed by the heavy dragging of the satellite.

"Red alert, Patsy."

They scrambled out and followed, hurrying from doorway to waste bin, waste bin to behind-the-corner, behind-the-corner to behind-somebody's newspaper. The gang were led out of the terminal building, and onto the vast, open stretch of concrete which led, in turn, to the airport's runways.

From around the corner of the terminal building came an unmarked aeroplane, its jet engines shrieking, ready for take-off. It was much smaller than those used to take tourists on holiday. Jeremy, concealed by a security patrol car, estimated it would seat about two dozen people.

"So with Mammoth and Mammoth II: The Sequel in there it'll be quite a squash," yelled Patsy above the din.

The plane taxied slowly around in a wide circle. The howling of the engines rose and fell as it manoevered. The mysterious figure stepped forward, holding his hat onto his head, and beckoned to the gang. A door in the side of the plane swung open, and a short stepladder dropped out. It was soon fixed, and the villains boarded the plane. At least, two of them boarded the plane, the other two sort of squeezed in painfully, grunting and wriggling.

"Now! We can't let them get away!" yelled Jeremy.

The door began to close, and the plane began to glide towards the runway. Patsy broke cover and dashed towards it. Jeremy broke cover and decided to try something else, because dashing after a plane just seemed like too much effort.

A security guard approached the patrol car they'd been hiding behind, and hopped into the driver's seat. Jeremy hopped in beside him.

"Follow that plane!" he ordered.

"I can't do that," said the guard, "I'll be in trouble."

The plane was getting further away. Patsy's trainers pounded the tarmac. Her face was redder than her hair, and her arms shifted faster than a fresh batch of hot cakes.

"Quick!" said Jeremy. "Follow that plane!"

"Ooo, are you a secret agent or something?" said the guard, excitedly.

"I can't tell you that, it's a secret!"

"Oh, go on, don't be rotten."

The plane's engines were picking up speed. "Just drive!" yelled Jeremy. The guard drove. "You're not like those other guards, are you?"

"No," said the guard sadly, "we don't get on."

The patrol car drew level with Patsy. If she'd been able to spare the time and energy to make a rude sign at Jeremy, she would have.

Faces appeared at the plane's windows. Sid looked horrified and shouted something to the pilot. The two Kenneths squashed their noses against the glass and puffed out their cheeks.

Patsy leaped fowards, flinging herself onto the plane's wing. Her legs flapped madly as she fought to keep a grip on the smooth surface.

Jeremy clambered out onto the roof of the patrol car. The wind blew his hair into a frizzy mass, but there was no time to worry about that now. The guard swerved the patrol car nervously as Jeremy steadied himself, and jumped.

He skidded across the wing. The plane was veering left and right in an effort to shake them off. Patsy caught his collar as he began to slip backwards. "Didn't I say I always have to save you?" she grumbled.

The door in the side of the plane *kss-chunged* as it unlocked and swung open. Kenneth (they couldn't tell which one) filled the doorway. "Hallo," he said with a little wave, "nice to see you again."

Sid kicked him from behind. "No it isn't!" he hissed. "Tell them to buzz off!"

"Buzz off," said Kenneth.

"No!" said Jeremy defiantly.

"So be it," said Sid. His cackle was almost as loud as the engines. The door shut and bolted. The plane picked up speed, moving out onto the runway. It accelerated, faster and faster.

Jeremy and Patsy gripped the wing with all their strength. Their eyes were tightly shut against the wind. The runway shot past under their feet. The whine of the engines rose higher and higher.

The plane's nose rocked slightly. The runway seemed to drop away beneath them. The plane banked steeply upwards. Their stomachs suddenly rolled over and did a couple of double somersaults that any Olympic gymnast would be proud of.

Kenneth and Kenneth watched calmly from inside. Second-Kenneth munched on a packet of wine gums. One day he'd learn to take the wine gums out of the packet first.

The plane gained altitude. Patsy's hands were frozen with cold and her face ached from being screwed up so hard.

"I— think—," she screamed at Jeremy, "when— they— said— buzz— off- you— should— have— said— YYEEEEESSSS!!"

CHAPTER FIVE

**In which everybody gets duffed up
and our heroes face certain death**

Inside the plane, Sid dodged this way and that to see around the Kenneths. "What are they doing?" he said. "Why aren't they falling off?"

"That ginger lass is a strong 'un," murmured First-Kenneth to his brother. "I'd like her to be my girlfriend."

"Get out on that wing and throw them off!" spat Sid. "We've come too far to let a couple of do-gooders spoil things!"

He turned, grinning weakly and bowing to The World's Sneakiest High-Tech Bad Guy, who was sitting at the far end of the cabin. "Don't you agree, your most wonderful nastiness, sir, your highness, m'lud?" squirmed Sid. The Bad Guy smiled a dreary smile.

Sid unlocked the door and flung it

open. Howling blasts of air suddenly filled the cabin.

Moments later, two huge, heavy shapes thumped onto the wing in front of Jeremy and Patsy. The plane suddenly spun to one side, the weight of all four of them pulling it over.

The Kenneths screamed for their mum. The ground, far below them, appeared to flip up and round and over their heads, and up and round and over as the plane rolled. Jeremy and Patsy screamed too.

The Kenneths, holding on tightly, struck out. A fat palm smacked against Jeremy's shoulder and he let go with one hand. He fluttered like a shirt on a washing line. Patsy ducked to avoid a flying fist. She thought she could hear one of the Kenneths shouting to her about going out for a pizza sometime, maybe, but decided she must be going barmy.

The plane stabilised, but on its side. The weight of the Kenneths kept the wing they were all on pointing downwards, with the other wing sticking up vertically. Patsy glanced down for a second, then wished she hadn't. They were about 10,000 feet off the ground.

A fat fist smacked against Jeremy's fingers. Luckily, his fingers were so cold by now that the blow wasn't too painful, and he managed to hang on. Then a boot squashed into his face. His fingers were at full stretch. His mouth twisted sideways as Kenneth's boot pushed harder.

Patsy's grip was being reduced one bit at a time. First-Kenneth grabbed each of her fingers in turn and pulled them off the surface of the wing. "One little piggie went to Margate..." called First-Kenneth. "One little piggie sat in foam..."

Jeremy yelled as loud as the boot would allow. "Hey, boys! Who wants an ice cream?!"

The Kenneths both raised their hands, and tried to jump up and down in excitement. Then they realised they were trying to jump up and down in mid-air. They found themselves watching the ground getting closer and closer.

With the weight gone, the plane flipped through one hundred and eighty degrees. Jeremy and Patsy's grip on the wing finally gave out and they fell, but with the plane now the other way up, they fell straight back through the door. The aircraft twisted again and flew level.

Wind whipped around the cabin. Jeremy and Patsy painfully untangled themselves from the Eazee-Rest reclining chairs, and stared up into Sid's weasley face.

"Oh, I'm really, really unhappy now," said Sid quietly.

Jeremy clambered to his feet and tried to look dignified. "I order you to turn this plane around and return to the airport."

"Shan't!" said Sid.

"Since they refuse to let us dispose of them," said a weary voice from the other end of the cabin, "they will have to come with us. We have many friends where we're going. They won't escape all of them."

Both Jeremy and Patsy knew that voice instantly.

There were lots of reasons why Jeremy liked being a secret agent. There was the thrill of bringing dangerous villains to justice, there was the joy of not being at school. There was also, now and again, the chance to be totally and completely gobsmacked by something. As the owener of the voice stood up and stepped forward, Jeremy could honestly say that his gob had never been more smacked. That mysterious figure at the airport had been Sharkface – 100% definitely. However, The World's Sneakiest High-Tech Bad Guy now turned out to be:

"Mr Tudor," said Jeremy.

"Crumbs," said Patsy, peeking over the back of a seat.

"You're not the only one with a secret identity," said Mr Tudor dolefully. "I've been studying online piracy for years, and with this" - he pointed to the satellite, strapped firmly into a chair - "I can hack into any system anywhere in the world. Nothing will be safe. Not banks, not building society current accounts. I'll have access to money, ANYbody's and EVERYbody's, whenever I want it."

Sid had read about this in the SCUM handbook - the big villain's revealing speech to the good guys, just before the end. He was filled with admiration. Then he frowned.

Just before… the end?

"Wait a minute!" he cried. "You're not getting MY money!" Wedged into the overhead luggage rack was the suitcase crammed with cash that Mr Tudor had given him in exchange for the satellite. The overhead luggage rack over Jeremy's head, as it happened. Jeremy yanked it free, intending to hold it up above him heroically, but it weighed a tonne. It thudded to the floor instead.

"Leave that alone, Brown!" cried Mr Tudor. "I plan to double-cross this little creep and steal it back!"

"WHAT??!" yelled Sid.

"You pushed me into a swimming pool, you oaf!" cried Mr Tudor.

Sid stamped his foot. "Aha! You're not wearing your woolly jumper! I'm telling your mum!"

Jeremy kicked the case over and gave it a shove. It slid to the very edge of the open doorway. Sid and Mr Tudor both dived for it at the same time. Patsy pulled off a shoe and flung it hard. It hit the case, the case toppled out into mid air, and the villains toppled out with it.

They fell trying to thump each other. The suitcase was snatched from one to the other and back again, as they vanished into tiny dots in the distance.

"I'm puzzled," said Jeremy, "That was 100% definitely Sharkface at the airport. Where did he go, then?"

"Look out!" yelled Patsy.

Sharkface sprang from the cockpit. He ripped a chair off its metal runners, and hurled it. They dropped to the floor and it crashed into the wall behind them.

"He's been the one piloting this

thing!" said Jeremy.

Sharkface ripped another chair up. "Huh? You're that snotty little Brown nobody from school," he grunted.

"And you're under arrest!"

Another chair smashed against the wall. Sharkface leapt at Jeremy. All Jeremy could think of was what had happened that morning on the way to school. He wasn't going to let it happen again. As Sharkface lunged for his throat, Jeremy ducked and rolled onto his back. Sharkface was going too fast to stop. He dived over Jeremy's head, and out through the door.

"Aha! Looks like that's that, then," said Jeremy.

Wrong.

The plane suddenly dipped sharply and went into a dive. The ground appeared through the front window, and the screaming of the engines rose to a deafening screech. Jeremy and Patsy tumbled forwards into the cockpit.

"Quick!" shouted Patsy. "Pull this

plane up straight!"

Jeremy jumped into the pilot's seat and strapped himself in. His fingers fluttered nervously over the dozens of switches and levers and displays in front of him. "Errr..."

"You can fly a plane, can't you?" said Patsy. "I mean, if Sharkface can do it... You must have done 'How To Fly A Plane' at MI7, surely?"

"That's next week," muttered Jeremy with a trembling voice.

"So this is it! After all that, we're still facing certain death!" This time, one of Patsy's doom-laden remarks looked like being completely correct.

Jeremy grabbed the joystick in front of him and pulled with all his strength. No response. He searched the displays for useful information. The ground was getting closer already. A red light above a row of other red lights blinked:

AUTOPILOT LOCKED. SECURITY CODE REQUIRED FOR RELEASE.

"They've made sure that if they

didn't make it," wailed Jeremy, "then neither would we!"

"Would breaking anything help?" said Patsy, hopefully.

"No no no! Get the satellite!" said Jeremy. "We've been chasing it around all day, the least it can do for us is a few sums!"

Patsy struggled back up the cabin, which was now almost vertical. The engines howled, and the rushing air made the remaining seats shake violently. She unstrapped the satellite. The second the buckle was unfastened, the weight of the thing sent her (and it) crashing back into the cockpit.

"Don't damage it!" yelled Jeremy.

Patsy would have given him a poke in the eye if she hadn't been pinned flat against the control panel. Jeremy opened several hatches in the side of the satellite, unwound the electric leads that fell out, and searched for a suitable socket on the plane's controls. "The good thing about technology," he mumbled, "is that these days you can…

A-hah!"

He plugged in. Patsy looked out of the window, then wished she hadn't. They can't have been more that five thousand feet off the ground now.

A screen came to life on the side of the satellite. As words appeared on it, a high, calm voice echoed them from a tiny speaker on the plane's control panel. "Initialising... Initialising..."

"Come oooon," mumbled Jeremy.

"Initialisation stage complete," said the satellite gently. "Status now being checked."

"We're going to crash!! That's our bloomin' status!!" bellowed Patsy.

"Patsy, be cool," said Jeremy, very, very worried indeed.

"Status check complete," said the satellite, calmly. "Altitude now 4,976 feet and falling... 4,532 feet and falling... 3,991 feet and falling... A change of course is recommended."

"Well do it, then!" shouted Patsy.

"You can't just tell it, Patsy," said Jeremy, "you have to program it."

"3,433 feet," said the satellite.

Clouds flashed past the windows. Patsy could make out buildings down below. Her stomach said a quick toodle-oo and tried to find the nearest exit. Jeremy tapped uselessly at the keyboard set into the side of the satellite. He wished he'd payed more attention during IT lessons.

"2,877 feet. Change of course required. Impact in seventeen seconds... sixteen... fifteen..."

"Shut up!!" screamed Patsy.

Jeremy clapped his hands to his head. He had to think. They both had to think. Thinking was the only way out.

"Twelve... eleven... ten seconds..."

"The satellite's monitoring the plane's controls now," murmured Jeremy quickly. "The controls are locked. If the satellite realises they're locked, it'll have to take over."

"Nine... eight... seven..."

Startled birds clung to the plane's nose, squawking. Patsy could see trees, fields, cars on the roads.

"Six... Five..."

Jeremy pushed hard on the joystick. The satellite bleeped.

"Controls are disabled," it said soothingly. "Autopilot will be overriden. Safety program is running."

Suddenly, the plane's nose lurched upwards. Gravitational forces pulled Jeremy and Patsy tight into their seats. The plane swooped in a sharp U-shape. The tip of the left wing clipped a spray of leaves from a tree.

The sudden falling of a whopping great aircraft, and it's lightning manoevers back up into the sky, were watched by a nearby flock of sheep. They chewed casually, their eyes following the movement.

As the plane automatically banked and headed back to the airport, Jeremy took out a hanky, mopped his brow, and had clearly forgotten all about the 'How To Stop Shaking Like A Leaf' lesson MI7 had given him.

"Looks like I've saved the day again," he said cheerily. Patsy scowled at him, but he took no notice. "Did I ever tell you about the time I fooled a Russian assassin into thinking he was a small dog called Arnold?"

"Yes," said Patsy, crossly.

Concerned and sensitive readers will be pleased to hear that none of those ejected at 10,000 feet ended up as blobs of strawberry jam on someone's front doorstep. As the plane came safely into land, Sid, the Kenneths, Mr Tudor and Sharkface were crawling out of the sludge tanks at the sewage works and into the welcoming arms of the local police.

Jeremy and Patsy retured home. They trudged up the street towards their respective houses.

"I'm going to have a bath," said Jeremy. "I'm going to put my hideously stained school uniform in the wash, and I'm going to prepare a new chapter for my memoirs, entitled 'I Foiled Crime At 10,000 Feet.'"

Patsy said something very rude indeed, but Jeremy wasn't listening.

There was a buzzing sensation in his left thumb...

THE END

JEREMY BROWN AND THE MUMMY'S CURSE

CHAPTER ONE

**In which Jeremy Brown shakes with
fear and a mummy comes to life.**

Jeremy Brown's secret was safe. Everyone at Grotside School thought of him as that weedy kid with the glasses. Only his best friend Patsy Spudd knew that underneath this clever disguise, he was an MI7 agent. And a rather brilliant one at that, he always thought.

Of course, if he'd paid the same attention to his school work as he did to catching crooks and saving the world, he'd have already got twelve A-levels, and a degree from the University Of Brains. As it was, he came bottom in everything, unless Patsy beat him to it.

It was Friday afternoon, double Maths with Mr Algebra, and everyone was fed up.

"I'm fed up," mumbled Patsy, too fed up to say anything more original.

She kept wrapping her ginger hair around her fingers.

Mr Algebra wrote a set of formulas on the blackboard. If Jeremy had been paying attention, he'd have realised that they were perfect for helping to decode electronic locking systems. But he wasn't. Instead, he was thinking about his last mission, and how very clever he'd been in proving that diamonds were being smuggled out of the country by a little old lady from Swanage.

"Who'd have thought it," said Jeremy. "Hollow teeth."

"It was me who extracted them," said Patsy. "She might have been ninety-seven, but she still kicked like a mule," she added, rubbing her left leg.

The class stared vacantly at the blackboard with droopy eyes and ever droopier mouths. Some of them were bored to tears (and were wringing out their hankies), some of them were bored stupid (and had forgotten their names). Luckily none of them had been bored to death yet.

"I wish MI7 would call me with a case," muttered Jeremy. Very soon, he'd be wishing he hadn't said that. And to find out why, we must first go to Cairo...

The Egyptian museum was dark, silent and smelt of old socks. It was the smell of thousands of years of ancient history. Mummy cases lined the walls, and huge stone statues of gods and animals stood in every corner.

The last visitor of the day had left hours ago. Agent Spanner of MI7 wandered along the upper gallery of the main hall, keeping a sharp eye out for something he knew was there, somewhere. His footsteps echoed around the walls. He was wearing a smart white suit, which is probably the silliest thing you can wear in a hot climate like Egypt's, but he'd seen people wear them in films on TV, so he reckoned he looked cool.

He dabbed the sweat off his forehead with his sleeve. It left a grubby stain. At last, he stopped in front of a particularly large, coffin-like and scary-looking wooden sarcophagus. It was covered in ancient Egyptian hieroglyphics, and a large, noble face was painted near its top in black and gold. Agent Spanner gulped quietly. "The casket of Psidesalad II," he whispered.

With both hands gripping one edge of the lid, he heaved the mummy case open. It creaked and groaned. A scattering of dust puffed out and settled nervously around his feet, glad to be out of there.

The mummy, its arms folded across its chest, stood tall and terrifying before him. It was wrapped tightly in bandages, and the bandages were wrapped tightly in dirt.

"Eurgh, it's a bit mucky," he mumbled to himself.

A thin beam of blue light ran from one side of the case to the other, level with the mummy's knees. Carefully, Agent Spanner reached out and broke the beam with his fingers.

His scream of fright was, just at that moment, the loudest noise in Cairo. The mummy's tightly encased hands had jerked into life. With sudden, sharp movements it grabbed the sides of the case and hauled itself forward.

Agent Spanner jumped back. The mummy's feet landed with twin thuds on the stone floor. He jumped back some more. The mummy stood up straight, towering over him. Agent Spanner would have liked to jump back roughly as far as France, but he was now pressed tightly against an exhibit of primitive farming tools.

The mummy closed in. Agent Spanner's eyes bulged out of his face like golf balls sitting on a pizza...

Jeremy's eyes were also bulging. He'd fixed his lids open with sticky tape in an effort to look alert, but all it was doing was making his eyes water.

"Did I tell you about the time I had to glue my knees together to prop a bank vault door open?"

"Many times," sighed Patsy.

Suddenly, Jeremy's tie began to make a tiny beeping noise. He sat up straight, wide awake. The rest of the class turned to peer sleepily at him. Mr Algebra craned his neck and shuffled from side to side. "Brown? Are you emitting a peculiar noise?"

Jeremy thought quickly. "Err, yes sir. It's my lower intestine. Very embarrassing personal problem, sir. Could erupt any minute."

Mr Algebra shuffled in horror at the thought of his lovely classroom awash with... "Quick! Get out! Find the school nurse! Or a toilet!"

"Thank you, sir," said Jeremy. All but one member of the class giggled cruelly as he dashed for the door. The odd one out was, of course, Patsy. She knew very well what that beeping meant.

Outside, in the chalky corridor, Jeremy quickly checked that nobody could see him. He stuck one end of his tie into his ear (the end with the miniature speaker in it), and held the other close to his mouth (the end with the miniature microphone.)

"The fairy cakes are made of sponge," said the deep voice of his boss at MI7.

"With big red cherries on the top," responded Jeremy correctly. "Morning, boss."

"Good morning, Agent Brown. Pay attention. A week ago, we lost contact with one of our overseas operatives, Agent Wrench. He'd been sent to Egypt, to guard an exhibition of relics on loan from the British Museum. After several days of silence, we sent a second operative, Agent Spanner, to track him down. Spanner discovered local reports of an ancient curse, which Agent Wrench had apparently fallen victim to."

Jeremy was starting to get a sinking feeling. "And what happened then?"

"No idea. Spanner vanished too. Swallowed up by the curse of the pharaoh Psidesalad II, by all accounts."

"Oh." It was at this point that Jeremy began shaking with fear, as mentioned at the start of the chapter.

"Your mission," continued the boss, "is to go to Egypt, find out what's going on, and stop it."

"I see... Err, wouldn't this be better tackled by... someone... a bit... taller, maybe?"

"Sorry, Brown. Every other agent is off on a training exercise, How To Confuse Your Enemies With A Garden Hose. You're the only one left. Operation Exit will be launched, as normal."

Jeremy's secret radio beeped, spluttered, and switched off. Moments later, the bell for the end of the lesson shattered the silence, not to mention his nerves. Patsy appeared at his side.

"I take it we're off?" she said eagerly.

His everyday disguise was pointless once more. Time for Jeremy to stop looking weedy and scruffy and start looking all heroic and smart. He straightened his tie, pulled up his socks and put on his special eagle-eyed look. Then he gave Patsy a quick summary of the situation. "MI7 chose me specially," he said. "The others all wanted the job, but there's only me brilliant enough to tackle it, of course."

"We're off, then!" grinned Patsy.

Operation Exit, meanwhile, involved MI7 telephoning the Headmaster of Grotside School. He was told that he should sign a letter allowing both of them to be out of lessons for as long as they wanted, otherwise the world would get to hear about his visits to the Peter Pixie Dressing Up Club.

Jeremy and Patsy collected their letter from his trembling hands on the way out of the school gates, and hurried to the airport. They flew to Cairo in the time it takes to start a new chapter.

CHAPTER TWO

In which Jeremy, Patsy and a camel are shot at with poison darts.

It was hot. Very, very hot. Think of the wave of heat you get when the oven door is opened. It was hotter than that.

"Oooh, it's hot," said Jeremy. He and Patsy had taken a taxi from Cairo Airport. After the taxi driver made them give it back, they'd caught the bus. They had now arrived at a busy, dusty, noisy, and quite amazingly hot bus station, outside the famous Museum Of Antiquities.

Patsy had remembered to bring her wide-brimmed sun hat, and had it jammed tightly on her head. Jeremy had to keep squinting. A short, round man wearing trendy sunglasses, and what looked like an enormous nightshirt, came bustling out of the museum.

"You make one tiny joke about

nightshirts," whispered Jeremy to Patsy, "and you're on the next plane home. It's called a gallibiyya. Traditional dress in this part of the world."

The round man shook their hands warmly. "I'm Mustafa Hapu," he said, with a broad grin. "I'm in charge of the British Museum exhibits while they're here in Egypt," he said.

"Lovely to meet you. I am Jeremy Brown of the Secret Service," announced Jeremy in his most official-sounding voice. "And this is my Operations Co-ordinator, Patsy Spudd."

CrunCHH-chomp!

Patsy spun around, ready to thump whoever had just snatched her hat away. She found herself staring up into the face of a dopey-looking camel. The last shreds of her hat were just vanishing between its teeth.

"This is my camel, Deidre," said Mustafa Hapu proudly. "Say hallo, Deidre."

Deidre snorted loudly at Patsy. Patsy wiped her face clean, grumbling rudely under her breath.

"I named her Deidre in honour of my favourite aunt," said Mustafa.

"Why, does your aunt like camels?" asked Jeremy.

"No, she just looks like one," said Mustafa. "MI7 informed me you'd be arriving. In view of the fact that the curse of Psidesalad II has already gobbled up two of your agents, I have arranged a bodyguard for you."

Two pairs of piercing, narrow eyes darted into view, behind which lurked Mustafa's henchmen, Aten and Amun. They too wore long, flowing gallibiyyas. Patsy thought they looked like they'd both sell their grannies for half a dozen trading cards and a jam doughnut. Jeremy just thought they were terrifying.

"Hallo boys," he said, with a polite but wobbly smile.

Aten and Amun bowed low, and said nothing. It was lucky that their bows almost brought their noses to ground level, because otherwise they'd have been hit by the poison darts which now flew over their backs.

Patsy kicked Jeremy hard on the hip, and he was thrown sideways. The darts missed his shoulder by millimetres and embedded themselves into the side of a passing wooden cart.

"Oww!" yelled Jeremy.

"You'd have been oww-ing worse than that if they'd hit you!" said Patsy. "Look!"

As the cart disappeared into the crowds, they could see that the wood around the area where the darts had struck was turning black.

"Poisoned," said Jeremy quietly. "Where did they come from?"

Phhh-eeoooo! Phhh-eeoooo! Two more darts bounced off the pavement by their feet. Aten and Amun were suddenly nowhere to be seen. Mustafa Hapu was spinning on the spot, looking this way and that.

Jeremy remembered what he'd read in MI7's brochure 'How To Spot Trouble'. He quickly analysed his surroundings: lots of people, lots of cars, and three really enormous camels. Much bigger then Deidre. And sort of... shiny-looking!

The head of one of the big camels suddenly swivelled round. Its perfectly circular eyes zoomed in on him. Where there should have been pupils, there were cross-hairs, like the rangefinder of a gun. The camel's head jutted forward. Slots slid open across its nostrils.

Phhh-eeoooo! Phhh-eeoooo! Jeremy dropped to the dusty pavement. The darts whizzed over his head.

"They're after US!" he yelled at Patsy.

Patsy began to make a dash for it, but there was too much traffic. Every direction was blocked with people, buses, taxis, carts and market stalls!

Phhh-eeoooo! Phhh-eeoooo! Smack into the front tyre of a bicycle. The rider pitched over into the back of a truckload of manure, which carried him away with his legs wriggling wildly in the air.

A dart could hit one of the crowd

at any moment! Jeremy had an idea.

"Mustafa!" he called. "Can we borrow Deidre?"

Mustafa Hapu had taken cover under *Ibrahim's Pet Parade* stall, behind a sign saying 'Little Birdies, Going Cheap.' His hand poked out in a quick thumbs-up sign.

The three big camels were marching through the crowd, heads turning, target sensors homing in on Jeremy and Patsy. Their legs whirred and ka-clunked as they walked.

"Are they what I think they are?" whispered Patsy.

"Yes," said Jeremy. "Robot camels with nasal armaments!"

Patsy jumped up onto Deidre's back, and hauled Jeremy up after her. She tugged on Deidre's ears. "Move!" she bellowed. Deidre lurched and bucked.

The robots instantly turned to pursue them, walking faster.

Deidre, not being the most intelligent animal in the world, bounded ahead in a straight line, which meant going right over the roofs of the cars. Jeremy and Patsy hung on as best they could. Deidre crunched her way across one vehicle after another, closely followed by various shouts, raised fists and threats of a thump in the face.

The robots increased their speed. They took a different approach with the traffic. They kicked it out of the way. A taxi was hurled over the railings of the museum. The fleeing crowd was splattered with bits of squashed fruit from a shattered cart.

Patsy tugged on Deidre's right ear, and the camel took a sharp turn down a narrow alley lined with shops. The way ahead was more or less clear, and Deidre got up to a full gallop. The sound of cars being crunched was close behind them.

Back in the street, an enormous lorry, carrying rocks, skidded and crushed one of the robots under its wheels. The robot's casing split, showering the street with sparks and circuits. The remaining two ignored it.

They turned right, down the alley.

Jeremy took a quick glance back. The robots were galloping too, and much faster than Deidre. They'd catch up in seconds. Their heads jutted forward, and their nostrils whirred open.

"Who's controlling them?" shouted Patsy.

"I could make a couple of guesses," shouted Jeremy, "but right now I'm more worried about the—"

Phhh-eeoooo! Phhh-eeoooo!

Darts buzzed through the air. Jeremy and Patsy dodged left and right, gripping tightly onto Deidre's tough, shaggy coat (which was so tough and shaggy that darts simply bounced off it). Deidre galloped as fast as she could, her tongue lolling out. Her wet, slobbery lips flapped in the wind.

Phhh-eeoooo! Phhh-eeoooo! Darts struck the canvas awnings of some of the shops. Shoppers and shopkeepers dived out of the way. The robots moved faster, and faster. Jeremy could smell the engine oil in their joints.

Oil! Something slippery! Jeremy looked ahead up the alley, which wasn't easy with Deidre bumping and weaving all over the place. There was a large stall selling shampoo and soap.

"Patsy!" called Jeremy. "Hair gel!"

"Can't you forget your bloomin' hair for once?" cried Patsy. Then she realised what he meant. She gave a sharp nod, held on extra tight around Deidre's neck with her legs, and flung herself sideways. As they shot past the stall, she reached out and plucked off a jumbo-sized tub of gel. The weight of it almost dragged her under Deidre's thundering feet. She grunted and struggled, and pulled herself back upright, and quickly handed the tub to Jeremy.

A dart peee-owwed through the shoulder of Jeremy's school blazer, turning a little patch of it black. Now he was REALLY cross. Taking aim as accurately as possible (not at all accurately, in the circumstances), he flung the tub of gel.

It spun in a neat arc, and burst with a sloppy *SPLOPP* on the ground. The robot that was bringing up the rear stepped straight in it. Its legs buckled and slipped. It flipped helplessly heels over head, smacked into a wall and exploded in a deafening clap of thunder and a ball of flame.

The other robot ignored it, and carried on running.

"I bet this sort of thing never happens to the tourists around here," grumbled Patsy.

A group of thirty-two tourists, on a package tour organised by Sun & Sand Holidays Ltd, were at that moment enjoying a leisurely sightseeing cruise down the River Nile. The Sun & Sand representative was speaking to them slowly and calmly:

"So here we are, on the Nile, in the centre of bustling Cairo, the capital of Egypt. On your left, fishing boats known as feluccas. On your right, busy streets full of shops where you can buy souvenirs and..." (a puzzled pause) "...camels?"

The tourists turned, curious. Sure enough, a camel, carrying two Europeans, had just shot out of a narrow alley...

"There's the river!" shouted Jeremy. "We can short-circuit that last camel!"

Patsy grinned gleefully. She was going to enjoy this bit.

The last robot was right behind them. Darts rained down around Deidre's feet.

The tourists watched silently as a real camel, followed by a robot one, leapt at high speed off the tall bank of the Nile. The real camel hit their boat feet-first. The robot tumbled into the water.

The weight of the real camel smashed through the seats, smashed a hole in the boat's bottom, and deposited Jeremy and Patsy on top of the Sun &

Sand representative. The boat sank. Mrs Bedsit (from Hull) screamed at the top of her voice. Mr Bungalow (from Leamington Spa) was knocked unconscious by a lump of flying robot.

The water flooded the robot's gears and blew all its circuits. Like the boat, it quickly sank out of sight.

"I think we gave those camels the hump," said Jeremy.

Deidre doggie-paddled, or rather camel-paddled, to the shore. The tourists demanded their money back.

CHAPTER THREE
In which darkness falls, and so does a sarcophagus.

Two hours later, four things had happened. 1) Deidre had been returned to Mustafa Hapu safe and sound. 2) News of the camel attack had spread, creating fearful whispers throughout Cairo about the curse of Psidesalad II. 3) The sun had set, and long, black shadows had crept through the streets, beneath a sky streaked with a fiery red. 4) Jeremy had put on a clean shirt.

Mustafa had found Jeremy and Patsy rooms at the remarkably large and remarkably shiny Pyramids Palace Hotel. They checked in wearing dark glasses and false beards, using the fake identities Mr N.Code and Miss D.Cypher.

"Lucky I'm a master of disguise," said Jeremy. "Nobody will guess we're undercover agents now. Whoever sent the robot camels after us might be searching the hotels, so we must be careful."

They had dinner in the hotel's remarkably posh restaurant, keeping out of sight behind their menus. Jeremy had a mix of traditional local dishes - mazzah to start, then kusheri and fattah, followed by baklava. Patsy had pie and chips.

"I can't take you anywhere," grumbled Jeremy.

"I like chips," hissed Patsy through gritted teeth.

With the moon high in the sky, they made their way to the museum. Mustafa had leant them a key. Jeremy wasn't keen on wandering around a dark and mysterious old building in the middle of the night, especially when there were ancient curses lurking about the place. However, Patsy called him a big weedy weed, and he changed his mind.

The huge, wooden front door shut with a clangorous thud behind them.

The sound echoed off the massive stone pillars that rose up high into the gloom, then faded away among the statues and glass cases. Jeremy switched on the torch they'd also borrowed from Mustafa.

"This place smells of old socks," mumbled Patsy, wrinkling her nose up.

Jeremy examined a small figurine of a jackal-headed god. "Should have paid more attention in History," he said. "Now then, time to bring my simply enormous brainpower into play and find some clues."

Patsy pulled an uh-oh-here-we-go face. Jeremy pretended he hadn't seen.

"Do we have a clear idea of exactly what's going on?" he said.

"No," said Patsy.

"Have we got any firm leads on what might have happened to Agent Wrench and Agent Spanner?"

"No," said Patsy.

"So, we're not doing too well, so far, are we?"

"No," said Patsy.

A sharp beam of torchlight wobbled ahead of them as they tiptoed around the displays, up a wide, stone staircase, along a narrow corridor, through a room filled with manuscripts, past a model of an Ancient Egyptian village... and realised they were completely lost. Then they remembered the map that they'd also borrowed from Mustafa, and soon arrived at the tall, vaulted gallery where the mummy cases stood.

Jeremy ran the torch beam up and down each case. They didn't get much of a look at the beautiful designs and skillful carvings on them, because Jeremy's hand was shaking with fright.

"Oh, give it here," said Patsy, pulling the torch away from him. Then she whispered "This one over here must be one of the exhibits from London. This is the sarcophagus of Psidesalad II."

Jeremy gazed up at it, eyes nearly as wide open as his mouth. "How do you know?" he breathed. "Can you read the hieroglyphics on the casing?"

"No, I can read the label on the side which says 'Property Of The British Museum.' Shine the torch here, along the floor."

There were footprints and marks in the dust, all over the wooden boards. Hundreds of visitors had passed this spot in the last few days, but Jeremy picked out two sets of prints which came closer to the sarcophagus than all the others.

"Look," he whispered. "One pair of ordinary sized feet, and one pair so big they'd make King Kong wet his pants. The ordinary feet jump backwards, away from the others, as if they're trying to escape." (These were Agent Spanner's footprints, as made in Chapter One.)

"How do you know they're going backwards?" asked Patsy.

"Because they go right up to this glass exhibit case, but they're facing away from it. Whoever it was - maybe Agent Wrench or Agent Spanner - clearly didn't walk through the glass case and towards the sarcophagus. The glass case is full and unbroken. So he must have been going backwards from the sarcophagus to the glass case. See?"

Patsy didn't. "You mean he came out of the sarcophagus?" she said, puzzled.

"No, the enormous footprints come out of the sarcophagus," said Jeremy.

They looked at each other for a second. Shivery sensations gleefully played football in their stomachs. Without a sound, Patsy shone the torch along the side of the sarcophagus. There wasn't a trace of dust along its edge.

"Recently opened," gulped Jeremy.

"We'd better take a look inside," said Patsy.

"We'd better call MI7 for back-up. Tanks, cars with sirens, that sort of thing."

"No time," said Patsy. She gripped the edge of the mummy case and heaved it open. It creaked and groaned. The torch lit up the tightly bandaged face of the mummy inside. Its arms were crossed over its chest, and it towered above them.

"Big bloke, wasn't he?" trembled Jeremy.

With a sudden rush of fear to the head, Patsy quickly slammed the lid shut again. As you may have guessed, she was a girl who was stronger than she looked, and the force of the slam made the whole sarcophagus wobble dangerously. Their efforts to stop its rocking motion only managed to make things worse.

"Jump!" yelled Patsy. "It's coming down."

They dodged sideways as the heavy wooden case hit the floor with a shattering crunch. It instantly split into a hundred pieces.

The shattering crunch's echo died away, and the dust began to settle. In the shaky torchlight, they could see the mummy lying face down in the debris.

Was that the sound of the broken pieces settling? Or were they being moved aside? Was that the moon throwing eerie shadows across the room? Or was the mummy trying to stand up?

"Oh crumbs," whispered Jeremy.

It was unmistakable now. With slow, jerky movements, the mummy was clambering to its feet. Pieces of sarcophagus were swept away with casual swats of its chunky, wrapped hands. As it reached its full height, it turned to face them. Its arms reached out for them.

"I think," said Patsy, "that this is the bit where we RUUUUUUNN!"

In their fright, they ran into each other, and various exhibits, as much as they ran for the exit. Not that they knew where the exit was any more - the map was somewhere under all that mess.

The mummy lurched forwards, straight at them. They turned a corner and found themselves in a long room lined with mummy cases. The sound of slow, heavy footsteps thudded in the darkness behind them.

"I've got a brilliant idea," said

Jeremy. "But it's yukky, so I won't tell you what it is."

"Hide in the mummy cases!" cried Patsy. "Brilliant!"

"Eurgh!" squirmed Jeremy.

"They're only dead bodies!" said Patsy. "Or would you rather be got by King Tut back there?"

They each chose a sarcophagus, and hauled the lids open. Leaping inside, however, was not an option. Bandaged arms instantly lunged at them. Mummies, every bit as huge as the first one, stepped out. The lids of the other cases in the room slowly creaked open.

Jeremy and Patsy turned and dashed back the way they had come. Then they realised that the first mummy was back that way, so instead they turned and dashed along the gallery which overlooked the main hall.

"This is where commando combat training comes in handy," gasped Jeremy.

"Yes. If only we'd had some," said

Patsy.

Fortunately, the stairs down to the hall were straight ahead of them. Unfortunately, up the stairs were coming half a dozen more mummies. Jeremy and Patsy skidded to a halt.

"Trapped!" said Patsy.

Jeremy leaned over the gallery's railings, looking down into the gloom of the hall. They couldn't simply jump over - too high. He ran over to the nearest exhibits: a statue that was far too heavy to move, a mummified cat, and an oar from an ancient boat.

The mummies closed in on both sides. The thumping of their enormous feet made the floor shake.

Jeremy grabbed the mummified cat and started to unravel its bandages. He tied one end around the railings.

"I hope this moggie was well fed," he said. "We need enough wrappings to climb down at least fifteen metres!"

Patsy quickly unwound the wrappings over the edge, tying loose ends together as she went. She nearly mentioned something about these strips of cloth being two thousand years old, and therefore unlikely to take their weight, but she didn't. She soon wished she had.

The mummies emerged from the shadows. They were barely an arm's length away. A mummy's arms's length, that is.

"Move!" yelled Patsy. Clinging on tightly, the two of them launched themselves over the railings, and dropped. Two of the mummies swung their fists, but only succeeded in hitting each other. The one closest to the railings was knocked over them.

Jeremy and Patsy fell until the cat's wrappings reached their limit and pulled tight. Sure enough, two thousand year old strips of cloth are complete rubbish when it comes to dangling in mid-air from a railing. They snapped instantly, but the sudden jerk that snapped them was also enough to break Jeremy's and Patsy's fall. They hit the stone floor of the main hall with a variety of painful thuds, but fortunately with no bones broken.

A falling mummy almost landed on top of them, making dents and cracks in the floor. Its innards made a crashing, coming-apart-at-the-seams noise. The bandages around its right arm came loose, revealing shiny metal beneath.

"They're robots too!" said Patsy.

"Thought as much," fibbed Jeremy. "I, err... never believed all that curse business, anyway."

The other mummies were now lumbering down the stairs. Jeremy and Patsy hurriedly untangled themselves from the heap of wrappings and bits of smashed robot that littered the floor. Without looking back - without looking anywhere, really, because it was especially dark down here - they scrambled for the front door.

The damage they caused by bumping into things and knocking them over was nothing compared to the damage caused by the mummies bumping into things and knocking them over.

With the sounds of pounding feet and disintegrating relics ringing in their ears, Jeremy and Patsy flung open the door and ran across the museum gardens. The mummies were still in pursuit, crowding through the door and spreading out to cover the grounds.

Jeremy and Patsy jumped onto the back of a passing horse and cart. Jeremy was relieved to find that it was carrying rolls of cloth, and not something smelly.

"Good evening," he called politely to the sleepy driver. "Could I possibly ask you to drive us away from here very, very fast indeed?"

The driver turned, rubbing his eyes. "Huh?" he grunted. Then he caught sight of the mummies. Pausing only for him to scream horribly, the cart shot away into the night.

CHAPTER FOUR

**In which Patsy is nearly sick,
and Jeremy uses his comb.**

The cup shook, and the tea in the cup shook in time with it, and all because Mustafa Hapu's hand was shaking too. As he held the cup delicately, his little finger poked out at an angle, and that was shaking worst of all.

Mustafa, Jeremy and Patsy were sitting on big, fluffy cushions, in a neatly ordered room in Mustafa's house. It was early the next morning. Patsy hadn't yet noticed that Deidre, (curled up on a carpet behind her), was nibbling at her hair. Household staff wandered back and forth, doing the laundry, tidying up, and listening in on the conversation.

"An interesting story, Mr Brown," said Mustafa, adjusting his sunglasses.

"It appears that our museum, our pride and joy, has been taken over by monsters."

"Robots," corrected Patsy.

"Still monsters in my book," said Mustafa. He took a nervous slurp of tea. Jeremy and Patsy did the same. "And I've learnt that they are beginning to move around throughout the city," he continued. "Nobody will take action against them. The power of the ancient curse is upon us."

"The power of MI7 will be upon us if we don't get to the bottom of all this," said Jeremy. "For a start, where are those two bodyguards you assigned to us?"

"Aten and Amun?" said Mustafa. "They vanished too. Right off the street, as you were chased by those evil camels!"

Deidre gave a shudder at the memory of them, and the shudder pulled a chunky tuft out of Patsy's hair. Patsy slapped her hands to the back of her head, and spun around, glaring.

Jeremy's eyes went all shifty, and his voice went all suspicious. "Of course," he said, "whoever is controlling the robots would want to make it look like THEY had vanished too."

Mustafa gulped down the last of his tea. "Perhaps you're right. I never quite trusted those two. Come, I have my helicopter on standby on the roof. The streets will not be safe."

"Hey, Patsy," said Jeremy. "Helicopters. Your favourite."

But Patsy wasn't listening. She was too busy fighting with Deidre on the carpet.

The sun beat down as the helicopter rose. Mustafa was the pilot, because he liked to be the one to say all that "Roger, over and out" stuff into the radio. Jeremy was beside him, binoculars at the ready. Patsy and Deidre were on the back seat. Patsy made rude signs at Deidre, and Deidre licked Patsy's face.

"I think I'm going to be sick,"

growled Patsy.

The helicopter swooped over Cairo. Mustafa liked to be the one to do all that swooping stuff, too.

They could see broad, flat roofs, tiny streets, the domes of the historic mosques in the old part of the city. And it was all a sandy brown colour. Jeremy scanned the city through his binoculars.

"It's very dark down there," he said. Patsy leaned over and took the lens caps off. "Ah, but I think I'm looking at a better angle now, a-hem. I can see... some people running... And over there I can see... some other people running... Mummies are after them... They're running towards each other... They've... run into each other... The mummies are still after them... They're scattering..." He put down his binoculars. "Isn't it interesting, watching the way they go in all directions like that?"

"I think they'd prefer it if we actually helped them," said Patsy, trying to clean Deidre's dribble off her face with a hanky.

"Quite right," said Jeremy. "We must map the robots' movements. Mustafa, time to do some more of that swooping stuff, if you'd be so kind."

"Brill!" said Mustafa, and set about banking and swerving the helicopter, first in one direction, then another. Jeremy peered through his binoculars at the streets below, and scribbled notes onto the back of his hand. Patsy clung to her seat for dear life. Deidre had a sneezing fit in Patsy's face.

"I really am going to be sick!" shouted Patsy, getting out her hanky again.

The helicopter swooped and dived, sometimes in order to fly over a new area of the city, but mostly because Mustafa was really enjoying himself. Jeremy kept a careful count of where mummies were to be seen (at regular intervals, every two or three streets), and in which direction they were heading (the same direction, on the whole). Before long, he came to the conclusion that they'd been set out to form—

"A barrier," he said.

The MI7 handbook 'Standard Sidekick Behaviour' advised that sidekicks should now make an interesting observation. However, Patsy was busy avoiding Deidre's bad breath by pressing her hands over her face, so Mustafa Hapu stepped in: "You mean they're protecting something?" he observed.

"Interesting," nodded Jeremy. "They're in a roughly semi-circular formation, and they're moving very slowly in that direction." He pointed ahead of them. "Which means that whatever they're protecting will be in THAT direction!" He pointed behind them.

Mustafa Hapu swung the helicopter around. Directly ahead of them now, rising high above the rooftops, were three gigantic triangles.

"The pyramids," murmured Jeremy.

"The pyramids don't need

protecting," said Mustafa. "They're big enough to look after themselves."

Jeremy got on with a bit of careful thinking. The helicopter flew out over the wide area of sand which separated the city from the pyramids. Deidre got ready for a really huge, nostril-cleaning sneeze.

Patsy shut her eyes tightly. "If we don't land NOW, I am GOING TO BE SICK!!"

The helicopter rapidly descended.

The group of thirty-two tourists, on a package tour organised by Sun & Sand Holidays Ltd, were at that moment enjoying a guided tour of the area around the pyramids. They hadn't been told about the patrolling mummies. They also hadn't got over having their river cruise ruined by falling camels in Chapter Two, but the travel company had persuaded them not to fly home and complain to the authorities. The Sun & Sand representative was speaking to them slowly and calmly:

"So here we are, next to the magnificent pyramids, one of the ancient wonders of the world. On your left, the giant sphinx, a human-headed statue of a lion. On your right, many charming little stalls where you can buy souvenirs and..." (a puzzled pause) "...helicopters?"

The tourists turned, curious. Sure enough, a helicopter was rapidly descending towards them. The violent downdraft caused by the helicopter's rotors blasted sand, souvenirs and tourists all over the place. The area was engulfed in a whirlwind. Mrs Bedsit (from Hull) screamed at the top of her voice. Mr Bungalow (from Leamington Spa) was knocked unconscious by a flying souvenir stall. The Sun & Sand rep began to cry.

Patsy leapt out of the helicopter, closely followed by Jeremy, who was a bit annoyed at the way the whirlwind kept messing up his hair. Deidre, not having thumbs, was unable to undo her seat belt, and so she stayed where she was. With a cheery wave, Mustafa guided the helicopter back up into the sky, and with a quick loop-the-loop vanished into the distance.

"Which pyramid shall we try first?" said Patsy.

"We must apply careful, deductive methods to the situation," said Jeremy, combing his hair. "Let's see... Eeny, meeny, miny, mo..."

They set off for the one in the middle. The others were a long way away.

"It's too hot to walk," grumbled Jeremy.

Behind them, the tourists were fighting their way out from under mountains of sand and bits of shredded souvenir stall.

"Wow," said Patsy.

The gigantically enormous shape of the pyramid rose way up high in front of them. It was made of massive stone blocks, each the size of a wardrobe. There were a number of openings at various points up the sloping side.

"Entrances to the tombs of the pharaoh and his queen," said Jeremy. "Originally, they were sealed up, but the passageways were excavated long ago."

"Wow," said Patsy.

Shielding his eyes from the dazzling sunlight, Jeremy craned his neck to examine the entrances. Patsy kept getting a nervous tingle down her spine. It might have been leftover plops of Deidre's dribble, but it was more probably a feeling of creeping unease.

"Better get a move on," she said "Those mummies could turn up at any minute."

"There!" said Jeremy, pointing to an entrance about half way up the pyramid. "They're in there. All the other entrances are worn at the edges, but that one's cut nice and sharp into the stone."

"So it must be new," said Patsy.

"Right," said Jeremy. "You know, sometimes my brilliance astounds even me!"

Patsy began to clamber up the stone blocks. Jeremy tried to think of a way to ascend without getting all hot and bothered, but he couldn't.

By the time they'd hauled themselves up level with the entrance, they were hotter and more bothered than Jeremy had dared fear. They looked back down, but that just made them feel dizzy as well. Up here, the breeze made spooky noises as it whistled around the stones, and probably would have pulled creepy faces too, if it had been able. They stared through the entrance into the pitch black tunnel ahead of them.

"A-a-after you," said Jeremy.

With a quick oh-for-goodness'-sake look, Patsy marched in. Jeremy tiptoed. What neither of them knew was that it didn't matter how they proceeded. They had already been detected by an electronic early warning system, and a trapdoor was being activated.

All they could see, as they edged

down the passageway, was a rectangle of sky slowly getting smaller behind them. They felt their way delicately along the smooth, cold walls. The floor was angled steeply downwards, and they could feel scatterings of sand beneath their feet.

"The robots must come in and out along here," whispered Jeremy.

"It seems pretty quiet at the moment," whispered Patsy. "Perhaps we can creep up behind them undetected."

"Yeah," whispered Jeremy. "Looks like they've underestimated our keen intelligence and fiendish cunning."

KA-CHUNGGGG!

"WhoaaaAAAAAAAAAaaaaaa!"

"WheeeeeaaaaEEEEEEEEEEE!"

That was the trapdoor.

CHAPTER FIVE

**In which the villains are unmasked,
and our heroes are done for, for sure**

"Begin second stage production line!"

The voice was low, echoing around the shadowy, cavernous chamber. It came from a speaker mounted on the wall, above a line of complex-looking machines. Jeremy and Patsy were rubbing whatever bits of themselves they'd bashed on the way down the metal chute which had been lurking under the trapdoor.

"I knew I should have worn standard issue MI7 padded underpants," said Jeremy, wincing.

Suddenly, a mummy appeared out of the shadows. They froze with fear, but quickly thawed out again when they realised that it wasn't interested in doing them any damage. It lumbered across to one of the machines, pressed a sequence of buttons, and pulled a small red lever. The machine shuddered and clunked into life, and was soon chugging away to itself, emitting the occasional hiss of steam. The mummy went on its way.

As their eyes got used to the dimness, Jeremy and Patsy could make out many such machines, arranged in rows. Between the machines trundled conveyor belts, carrying various mechanical components. In the centre of the cavern rose a series of thick pipes, feeding into a huge cone-shaped device, which was suspended above the floor, pointing down.

"It's a factory," said Jeremy. "And you don't have to be as fabulously clever as me to work out what it's making."

"How long do you reckon it'll take to make an entire robot army?" said Patsy.

"Better ask Aten and Amun," said Jeremy. "I'm convinced those so-called bodyguards are behind all this. Even

Mustafa said he didn't trust them."

"Well, now's your chance," said Patsy.

Jeremy turned in the direction Patsy was pointing. There were Aten and Amun, bound tightly with ropes, blindfolded, and gagged, in a glass-sided booth marked PRISONERS.

Jeremy began to suspect that he might possibly have been wrong.

"Oh. Well, err... Maybe they're bluffing," he said grumpily.

"Or maybe," said a smarmy voice behind them, "we've caught another pair of nosy parkers."

Jeremy and Patsy were surrounded by mummies. Above the mummies, standing on one of the chugging machines, were Agent Spanner, and Agent Wrench. Jeremy couldn't help noticing that their smart white suits had become terribly wrinkled and marked in the heat of the desert.

"Yes, well, I told Spanner to buy more practical clothes, but he wouldn't listen," slimed Agent Wrench. He sneered at the glass booth. "These two tracked down our robot camel storage depot, and now, Brown, you and your scruffy little friend can join them in the cage. It will then be lowered into a pit of fresh concrete, from which you may possibly be rescued in a thousand years or so."

"And just where are you going to get a pit of fresh concrete?" cried Patsy.

Agent Wrench wriggled a long finger, flipped a switch on the side of one of the machines, and with an electric hum, a door slid open in the floor. "Here's one I prepared earlier," he grinned, horribly. He turned to Agent Spanner. "Spanner, I'm going to check the production line. Get the mummies to deal with these two."

"Do I have to?" whined Agent Spanner. "Those mummies frighten the life out of me."

"Yes you do!" yelled Wrench. "What kind of a criminal mastermind are you, if you can't send a few do-gooders to a nasty death! Get on with it!"

He scurried away. Agent Spanner waved in the general direction of Jeremy and Patsy. "Umm, stick them in the concrete, mummies, if you don't mind, please," he said.

The mummies lunged, and grabbed our heroes. Jeremy and Patsy were sealed up in the glass booth, along with their bodyguards, before Jeremy could think of a single witty remark.

"We're done for, for sure," quivered Patsy.

"Err..." said Jeremy.

With a jerk, the booth was hoisted into the air. It shook violently, although it was mostly the prisoners who were doing the shaking. The oozy, grey rectangle in the floor was directly below them. The chain from which the booth was hanging was locked in position. The booth began to descend.

"I suppose shouting 'help' wouldn't do any good?" shuddered Patsy.

They soon established that bashing the glass with their fists didn't do any good either. The concrete grew nearer and nearer.

"Rock!" shouted Jeremy suddenly.

"Not yet," said Patsy, "it's still liquid."

"No! Rock the booth!" Jeremy flung all his weight against one of the glass sides. Patsy realised what he was up to and joined in. Aten and Amun were still blindfolded, so all they could do was wonder what on earth was going on. The booth swung. Jeremy and Patsy leaped at the opposite side. It swung back. The swinging motion got wider and wider until—

Sss-KRRRRRAsssSHHHHH!

—it smashed against one of the machines. The prisoners tumbled to the floor in a shower of glass.

A loudly warbling alarm sounded. Agent Spanner covered his ears. "Oh, do we have to have that awful din ever time something happens?"

Agent Wrench looked up from the computer console he was working at. His face twisted into something that would have given Dracula nightmares. "Catch them!" he spat at a nearby mummy. "And keep the production line going!"

Over by the shattered booth, Jeremy and Patsy were undoing the ropes around Aten and Amun. The bodyguards flung off their blindfolds and blinked nervously as they took in their surroundings.

"Never doubted you for a minute, boys," lied Jeremy. "You try to find a way out, and alert anyone you can find. Patsy and I will fight off the mummies, shut down the factory, arrest Agent Wrench and Agent Spanner, and... err... On second thoughts, y'know, finding a way out is more a job for a highly trained secret agent..."

But the bodyguards had already hurried away into the darkness. Jeremy and Patsy went in the opposite direction, towards the huge, upside-down funnel-thing in the centre of the factory.

Agent Wrench checked pressure gauges and electronic readouts, adjusted dials and operated switches. Agent Spanner was having a nice sit-down in the corner.

The noise of the machines rose. The conveyor belts moved faster. The central funnel shook, there was a loud KA-PING, and a fully-formed mummy dropped out with a crash. It stood up, its programming tuned it in to Jeremy and Patsy's location, and it moved off.

"Ha Ha Haaa Haaa HHaaaaaAAAAA Haaaa!" yelled Agent Wrench, and a few other things too. He slapped his hands together with glee.

"Honestly, there's no need to get so excited," mumbled Agent Spanner.

The funnel began to tremble again. Another mummy appeared...

KA-PING! Crash!

...and another...

KA-PING! Crash!

CHAPTER SIX

In which there is a colossal explosion

Meanwhile, Jeremy and Patsy had quite enough mummies to contend with already. The mummies weren't quite nimble enough to catch them if they kept crawling underneath the conveyor belts, so they followed the line of the machines back towards the centre of the cavern.

"I thought Wrench and Spanner were MI7 agents?" said Patsy.

"They are," said Jeremy. "Or they were. I've got a feeling they may possibly get the sack for this!"

"But what do they want an army of robots for?"

"Oh, come on Patsy, what would you do with an army of robots?"

"Ummm," pondered Patsy, "force the Headmaster to ban double Geography."

"Exactly," said Jeremy. "They could do whatever they want. Take over Egypt, MI7, anything. And if anyone moves against them, they just churn out more robots."

"Sounds like fun," said Patsy.

"Patsy!" cried Jeremy, shocked. "It's an appalling way to behave, and you know it! They're no better than playground bullies."

Suddenly, a bandaged arm swung out and grabbed Patsy's ankle. She twisted round and kicked with her other foot. Her boot clanged hard against the robot's ear. Its head bent inwards, sparks flew, and the mechanism holding her ankle let go.

"Looks like they've learned to crawl!" said Jeremy. They rolled out from under the conveyor belt and jumped to their feet.

Agent Wrench and Agent Spanner blocked their way ahead. Mummies blocked their retreat.

"Don't have to go just yet, do you?" said Agent Wrench, creepily. "We've hardly begun to make your lives a misery."

"Yes, you really are being a dreadful nuisance," added Agent Spanner.

Jeremy pulled himself up to his full height, which was about half Agent Wrench's. "You, mate, are a disgrace to the Secret Service. And so is your trained monkey here."

Agent Spanner fought back the tears. "I say we get really, really horrid with them," he quivered. "Straight away."

"Do you honestly think that disposing of us will stop you being found out?" said Jeremy. "MI7 will simply send in more agents."

Agent Wrench flung out his arms, grinning madly at the machines all around them. "By then it will be too late. Spanner's genius for electronics, and my genius for dastardly plots of international proportions, have created the ultimate weapon. Out here in Egypt, apparently on a mission, we could keep away from prying eyes while we build our factory. With the so-called curse of Psidesalad II to terrify and confuse everyone, we could test our robots in the field. We are ready for anything. Let MI7 send a hundred agents! We'll nobble the lot of them!"

"You're barmy," said Patsy.

"And you, Ginger, are history," sneered Agent Wrench. He turned to the mummies. "Attack!"

All hell broke loose. Things were thrown, shins were kicked, and bad guys got wrestled to the ground by Patsy. Jeremy dodged the fists of two advancing mummies. They ploughed into a machine, making mummy-shaped dents in it. Jeremy dashed over to Agent Wrench's computer console.

"Hold them off, Patsy, I'll try to shut down the production line!"

Mummies were hanging on to various parts of Patsy, trying to stop her wriggling. She had Agent Wrench's collar gripped tightly in one hand, and Agent Spanner's in the other.

"Gerrof," spluttered Agent Wrench, turning blue.

"That's not very nice, now, is it?" gasped Agent Spanner, turning purple.

Jeremy's hands fluttered over the banks of controls in front of him. He thought back to the MI7 'Stay Cool In A Crisis' lecture he'd been to. He examined the read-outs. He checked the dials. He made a calm, rational judgment about what codes he needed to tap into the computer to shut the production line off, and then pressed the ENTER key.

The production line speeded up.

Mummies started dropping out of the funnel at an alarming rate. They were coming at him from all directions, homing in on the intruder. Their arms reached out.

The conveyor belt next to Patsy was whizzing along now. Agent Wrench struggled wildly to free himself from Patsy's grip.

"Too fast!" he croaked. "It'll overload!"

With a whopping great SMACK, the conveyor belt buckled and snapped. One end whipped round and slapped a line of mummies into the air. The other end did the same to Patsy. Her scream as she was hurled upwards, clutching her bottom, is unrepeatable. She landed on top of the giant funnel, slipped, and only stopped herself falling by hanging on to the thick tubes which fed into the funnel's top. Several of them were split open, and jets of steam hissed in her face.

Jeremy watched helplessly. One mummy had both his arms, and another had both his legs. Luckily, all four limbs were still attached to his body. He'd worked out where he'd gone wrong at the controls, but there was no hope of having a second go. Agent Wrench and Agent Spanner were already hurrying over to the computer console, and making the adjustments needed to stop the machines overloading.

Patsy got another blast of hot

steam up her nose, and pulled out her hanky as a sneeze welled up. However, she'd forgotten that her hanky was still covered in the yukky mess Deidre had coated her with, during their flight in the helicopter.

"UUUrrrGGGHHggHH!" she cried.

Jeremy twisted towards her as best he could. "Patsy! I've got an idea! Stick that hanky in the funnel!"

Only too glad to get rid of it, Patsy stuffed the dripping hanky into one of the split tubes she was hanging on to. A sharp, blue crackle of power suddenly lit the tube from inside. She let go and dropped to the floor.

Agent Wrench and Agent Spanner stopped what they were doing. "NoOOooo!" yelled Agent Wrench. "You'll set the whole thing off! That slime will blow every circuit in it! My factory! My robots! My evil dreams of world domination!"

The machines shook and split. One by one, in a chain reaction, they exploded.

WHUMPPPHHH!
Ka-WHhhhoOOOM!
PHHoOOWWWW!

The group of thirty-two tourists, on a package tour organised by Sun & Sand Holidays Ltd, were at that moment enjoying an open-air lunch by the pyramids. They hadn't got over having their tour ruined by a helicopter sandstorm in Chapter Four, but the travel company had persuaded them not to demand their money back. Their tour bus was parked nearby, ready to take them back to their hotel. The Sun & Sand representative was speaking to them slowly and calmly:

"So here we are, before we depart for rest and relaxation by the hotel pool, enjoying a traditional meal cooked specially by a team of local chefs. On your left, freshly baked loaves of bread. On your right, many dishes made to ancient recipes and..." (a puzzled pause) "...a colossal explosion?"

The tourists turned, curious. Sure

enough, the top had blown off the nearest pyramid, and was shooting up into the sky. A deafening series of bangs sent a gigantic ball of smoke and fire billowing into the air. Blown out ahead of it all were four figures.

The tourists watched as the figures flew in a neat arc, up, over the desert, and down on top of their lunch. Jeremy and Patsy, their clothes and faces singed and smoking, crashed to an almost soft landing on the pile of bread. Agent Wrench and Agent Spanner skidded along the table, splattering food all over the tourists, and into the waiting arms of Aten, Amun, and the police.

Then the top of the pyramid arrived. By now, it had crumbled into a couple of dozen huge, heavy blocks, and the falling blocks smashed what was left of the tourists' lunch, tour bus and nerves. Mrs Bedsit (from Hull) screamed at the top of her voice. Mr Bungalow (from Leamington Spa) was knocked unconscious by a flying lump of stone. The Sun & Sand rep wet himself.

Jeremy dusted himself down. "Another job successfully concluded, Patsy," he said proudly. "The robots around the city should have switched off too, now their control system is gone."

They wandered out across the sand, paying no attention to the wailing of the tourists, the pile of rubble surrounding the tourists, or the dollops of hot food covering the tourists. Agent Wrench and Agent Spanner were already under arrest, in a police car half way to the airport.

"You know," said Jeremy, "when I write this up in my memoirs, I'll call the chapter 'How I Saved The World From Robot Domination, Single Handed.'"

Patsy, who'd had quite enough that day, spent a happy few minutes burying him upside down in the sand. But there was no time for mucking about. A beeping sound was coming from Jeremy's tie...

THE END

JEREMY BROWN
ON MARS

CHAPTER ONE

In which Jeremy and Patsy
travel several million miles

Grotside School, Thursday morning, about half past ten. Jeremy Brown, his best friend Patsy Spudd, and the rest of the class, were enduring the horrors of French with Madame Croissant.

"*Attention la classe!*" she squeaked from under her tight bun of hair, which always looked like it was nailed to her head. "*Et maintenant, nous alons etudier la leçon numero douze!*"

"How are we ever going to know what foreign words mean if she only ever talks to us in foreign?" muttered Patsy under her breath.

Jeremy shrugged his shoulders. He was busy thinking about his last case. The rest of the class thought of him as that weedy-looking kid with glasses, but the glasses and scruffy appearance were simply a disguise. A really brilliant disguise, too, he always thought, because nobody had the slightest idea he was an undercover agent for MI7. Nobody except Patsy, that is, and he sometimes wished she was in the dark too, because it meant she kept whispering things like:

"When are we off on another mission, then?"

"Shh!" said Jeremy. Madame Croissant was mercilessly brandishing irregular verbs. Anyone could fall prey to a grammar question at any moment.

"We haven't been called up since we solved the case of the Albanian ambassador's wooden legs," said Patsy.

"A fabulously clever piece of detective work on my part," said Jeremy, proudly. "Who would have guessed that they were being worked on strings by his dog?"

"It was me who blew the kneecaps off," grumbled Patsy.

Madame Croissant slapped her

hands together loudly. "*Ne parles pas en classe, Mademoiselle Pomme de Terre!*" she cried.

"Eh?" said Patsy.

"I wish we had another case," sighed Jeremy.

He'd regret saying that, because soon they would both be chased through an alien fortress by creatures with twenty-four tentacles each. To find out why, we must first shift back a few hours in time, to the previous night...

The British University for Monitoring Stars (which only very silly people ever called BUMS), stood tall, dark and silent. In the woods behind it, an owl hooted sleepily.

There were no lights to be seen at any of the building's windows. The only light at all came from the soft glow of the moon and the stars, and from the blinking of tiny bulbs on high-tech scientific equipment in the university's many laboratories. Everyone had gone home.

Except for one person. A shadowy figure was moving slowly along the main corridor on the fifth floor. The figure wore soft shoes, made no sound, and carried a large, black bag.

Silently, the bag was placed on the floor. Its zip was pulled back with great care. From inside was lifted a sleek, metallic device, about the size and shape of a laptop. It was set down next to the bag.

Small grippers suddenly sprung out from around its base and dug hard into the floor. Upwards from the top of the device whirred an antenna, at the tip of which flashed a tiny red light.

The stillness of the night was broken as the device began to emit a regular *bip-bip-bip-bip*, as it transmitted a homing signal. The figure gathered up the bag, moved swiftly to the lifts, and within minutes was out of the building and hurrying away. Up on the fifth floor, the homing beacon did its work.

The skies above the university

gradually filled with a weird humming sound that rose and fell in a particularly creepy way. Luckily, nobody was around to witness the scene, because while the humming was creepy, the strange way the stars appeared to be wobbling would have made any witnesses rush home to change their trousers.

Suddenly, there was a flash. A wide, red beam of energy short vertically out of the sky and slammed into the roof of the building, on a direct line to the position of the beacon inside. With a whopping great *WHOMPPPPHHH* every window shattered.

A second red lightning bolt hit the same position. The university's walls shuddered, tottered, and fell to bits in a rumbling tumble of concrete and dust. The wreckage settled into a giant heap, surrounded by swirls of what had recently been stairways and floors.

Slowly, with demolition complete, silence and darkness returned. The skies were peaceful, and the moon shone gently down on the rubble, as if nothing out of the ordinary had happened.

"Nothing out of the ordinary has been happening," sighed Jeremy. "That's the trouble. Oo! Ow!"

That 'Oo! Ow!' was caused by the sharp buzzing sensation he suddenly felt in his shoes. His shoes were where his secret MI7 communicator was hidden that day. MI7 was trying to contact him. Or else his feet had instantly grown three sizes bigger, but that hadn't happened since the case of the mutant Norwegians.

"Oo! Ow!" he winced again.

"*Vous avez un question, Monsieur Lebrun?*" squeaked Madame Croissant.

"No, Madame Croissant, I need to be excused. Err, lameness. It's hereditary. If I don't get medical attention immediately my feet burst and this horrible runny stuff comes out." He sprang up and hopped painfully to the door.

"*Non! Non! Non!*" squealed Madame

Croissant, rapping her ruler on the edge of her desk. "*En français! En français!*"

"Oh," said Jeremy. "Err, *je voudrais...* umm, *aller au...* Sorry, I haven't got time for this, really sorry."

He hobbled out, followed by an icy stare from Madame Croissant and a wave of cruel laughter from the rest of the class (except from Patsy, of course, who realised exactly what was going on).

"Oo! Ow!"

Outside, in the chalky corridor, Jeremy quickly checked that nobody could see him. He pulled off his shoes, held the heel of the left one up to his ear, and the heel of the right one up to his mouth.

"The blancmange is yellow," said the deep voice of his boss at MI7.

"Banana and pineapple flavoured," responded Jeremy correctly. "Morning, boss."

"Good morning, Agent Brown. Pay attention. Late last night, something caused the total destruction of the British University for Monitoring Stars."

"What, (smirk) you mean (snigger) BUMS?" chortled Jeremy.

"Only very silly people call it BUMS," snapped his boss. "A strange force reduced it to rubble in a matter of seconds."

"What sort of strange force?" said Jeremy nervously, getting the feeling that it would turn out to be something horribly dangerous.

"Evidence suggests a high energy beam fired from beyond Earth's atmosphere."

"Ah," said Jeremy, now pretty sure that it was something horribly dangerous. "Well, I'd love to help out, of course, but, umm, wouldn't this be best handled by an agent with more, you know, outer space experience?"

"We contacted all our agents with outer space experience," said his boss. "And now they're hiding under a table and won't come out. You're the only one left. Besides, the university is close to your school, so it'll save on travelling. Your mission is to discover the source of this energy beam, and put it out of action. Operation Exit will be put into effect, as usual. That is all."

The bell went for the end of *le leçon*. The corridor was filled with clumping boots and flying textbooks. Jeremy put on his shoes, took off his glasses, smartened his tie, and adopted his special secret agent cool look, which it had taken him ages to get right in the bathroom mirror at home.

Patsy didn't do anything to tidy herself up, because she preferred it that way. Her ginger hair looked like even a rat wouldn't have nested in it. "Are we off?" she said, excitedly.

"We're off," announced Jeremy. "They said the case was horribly dangerous, but I insisted on taking it anyway. First stop, the British University for Monitoring Stars."

"What, BUMS?" spluttered Patsy.

"Only very silly people call it BUMS," said Jeremy loftily.

Operation Exit, meanwhile, involved MI7 telephoning the

Headmaster of Grotside School. He was told that he should sign letters allowing Jeremy and Patsy to be out of lessons for as long as they wanted, otherwise the world would get to hear about his subscription to *Fluffy Bunnybears Monthly*.

Jeremy and Patsy collected their letters from his trembling hands on the way out of the school gates. They hurried off in the direction of what was left of the university.

What was left of the university was being clambered over by the people who, until the day before, had worked in it. They were salvaging what they could of the experiments they had been conducting, and the records they had kept, but all they were ending up with was a pile of shredded papers and battered equipment.

Jeremy and Patsy questioned one of the salvage team, and were directed to a tall man with a beard, who was wearing a sagging knitted cardigan and an expression of intense rage. The cardigan and the expression were an identical shade of mauve. This was the Head Of Research, Professor Killjoy.

"Good morning," said Jeremy politely, being careful not to get concrete dust on his trousers. "I am Jeremy Brown of the Secret Service, and this is my Field Tactics Manager, Patsy Spudd."

"Vandalism!" shouted the Professor. "Barbarism!"

"Oh dear," giggled Patsy, looking around, "someone's exploded your BUMS. It's (smirk, giggle) a bit of a 'cheek', really. Ha Haaaa!"

"Patsy, pack it in," said Jeremy crossly.

"You can both pack it in!" shouted the Professor. "I don't need smarmy know-alls like you to tell me it was those hooligans from Grotside School over there who did it! Arrest the lot of them! Now!"

A smooth female voice floated over the rubble. "Is that really a credible theory, Professor?"

The elegant Dr Nicely appeared. The surrounding area was tattered, devastated and ugly: Dr Nicely was the exact opposite. She held out a slender hand to Jeremy as she introduced herself.

"Do call me Heather," she purred, with a smile. Jeremy just grinned soppily and mumbled something about being delighted. Patsy made throwing-up noises. "The Professor is letting his emotions run away with him," said Dr Nicely. "This is the result of a directed high energy beam."

Dr Nicely was accompanied by her lab assistant, Wallingford Horatio Smith. The surrounding area was grubby, greasy and grey: Mr Smith was exactly the same. He scribbled notes on his clipboard.

"Do call me Mr Smith," he droned icily. "My colleagues are both wrong. This is due to freak earthquake activity."

"Balderdash!" shouted the Professor. "Twaddle!"

The three of them started up a heated debate on the causes of concrete crumbling and the exact nature of balderdash. Jeremy and Patsy looked at each other helplessly.

"Fat lot of use this bunch are going to be," said Patsy. "Still, at least they're not taking it 'sitting down'. Ha Haaaa! Can't be much fun having an energy beam right up their—"

"I do hope, Mr Brown," purred Dr Nicely, "that your friend won't be referring to the university as—"

"Good heavens no!" said Jeremy quickly, blushing. "Only very silly people do that. Come along Patsy, we must, er... search something."

"You could start in the woods over there," said Dr Nicely. "It would be an ideal place to hide the kind of very large mechanism needed to fire an energy beam of such power."

"What a perfectly perfect idea," said Jeremy, blushing again. "Do excuse us." He hurried Patsy away before she could say anything embarrassing.

*

They didn't find any large mechanisms in the woods. What they found was a door.

"At least, I think it's a door," said Jeremy.

It was tall, round and silvery, standing upright and on its own in a small clearing. Jeremy ran a hand across its surface. His voice went slightly spooky. "It looks metal, but it feels sort of like plastic. It's warm, as if it's powered up. And there are symbols pressed into it, all over. Look closely. That's not any language I've ever seen."

"Well, it's not French," mumbled Patsy.

Jeremy's fingers strayed across a rectangular panel in the middle of the door. It suddenly hummed loudly and the door slid back, revealing a swirling, greeny-grey vortex of light.

"Uh-oh!" said Jeremy.

"Hey, brilliant!" said Patsy. "Let's go through!"

If he'd had time, Jeremy would

have given stern warnings about the dangers of jumping into sinister, alien swirly lights. As it was, Patsy bounded in, dragging Jeremy after her. The vortex instantly transported them several million miles.

The door hummed shut.

CHAPTER TWO

**In which beings from a distant
world issue a very large bill.**

The room into which Jeremy and Patsy stepped was very long, very low, and very white. The transport portal door clicked and deactivated behind them as it closed.

"Crumbs," whispered Jeremy.

"Fantastic!" cried Patsy. The word bounced off the walls and wrapped itself back around their ears a few times. "Where are we?"

Their footsteps made echoey clacking noises as they walked forward slowly. Jeremy approached a wide rectangle set deep into one of the walls. Delicately, he reached out to the smaller rectangular panel at its centre. "I expect this opens the same way as that door," he said. "Logically, it ought to be the shutter for a window."

And so it was. As his fingers touched the panel, the whole thing slid upwards with a sharp hiss. Through the thick plexiglass was a vast landscape of dusty red plains and mountains, topped with a cloudless, pinky-purple sky.

"Good grief," whispered Jeremy, eyes wide.

"WwwoooooWW!" cried Patsy, squashing her face against the window and steaming it up with her breath. "It's another planet! It's a real life another planet! It's—"

"Mars," whispered Jeremy.

"WwwoooooWW!" cried Patsy again. "Time to explore!"

Jeremy looked back at the transport portal through which they had travelled. "Well, we know what's back that way," he said. "Let's see now..."

He wandered over to the far wall, which had an even bigger rectangle set into it. This one covered almost the entire end of the room, and reached from floor to ceiling. Once again, there was a smaller, rectangular panel at its centre.

"Logically, this ought to be a door," said Jeremy. "You know, it's lucky there's someone as clever as me around to work these things out. Did I ever tell you about the time I unlocked a safe during a six hundred metre plunge into a vat of blue paint?"

"Yes. Several times," mumbled Patsy.

"I just hope we don't encounter any terrifying alien nasties," said Jeremy.

He reached out and pressed the opening panel. Up hissed the door. Beyond it was an enormous control room, packed with weird machines, glowing displays...

... and terrifying alien nasties.

They looked at Jeremy and Patsy.

Jeremy and Patsy looked at them.

"Run!" yelled Patsy.

They made a dash for a long corridor which snaked away from the control room. All together, the aliens let out a spine-chilling, wailing screech and chased after them.

Patsy was in the lead, her stout boots ideal for running-away-type situations. Jeremy glanced over his shoulder. There were dozens of creatures right behind them. Each had a stumpy, round body, three eyes waving about on thick stalks, and twenty-four shivering tentacles which served as both arms and legs. They also smelt of cheese.

Jeremy thought they were utterly hideous and completely frightening. The aliens thought Jeremy was utterly hideous too, with his one nose and his four, jointed stick things. Unfortunately, he didn't frighten them one little bit.

"*Bok phaan parr'chak xa!*" howled the one closest to snagging Jeremy with a flying tentacle. Then the creature realised it hadn't got its translator turned on. It slipped a flat, grille-like device over its slit-like mouth and tried again: "Earthlings will halt! Earthlings are in violation of Rule 913, Paragraph 8, Subsection 2 of the Law Of Pursuit!

Earthlings will halt!"

"Hurry!" yelled Jeremy.

A loud, warbling intruder alarm started up. All the other aliens switched on their translators and issued information about the penalties for breaking the law.

Jeremy and Patsy's energy was beginning to sag. Jeremy made a mental note to eat a more nutritious breakfast in future. The smell of cheese coming off the aliens was making Patsy feel peckish.

They were running through an immense docking bay. Small, oval-shaped space vehicles were loaded into long, see-through tubes. The doors to the tubes were hanging open on chunky hinges.

"Escape capsules!" cried Jeremy, exhausted. "Patsy! Inside!"

"We can't fly one of them!" gasped Patsy.

"We can't escape this lot, either!" cried Jeremy.

Patsy dived through the miniature

airlock of the nearest capsule. Jeremy scrambled in after her. Quickly, they slammed the door shut behind them. Its thick locking clamps automatically ka-chunked into place. In seconds, dozens of alien tentacles were slapping angrily against it.

Jeremy and Patsy twisted uncomfortably in the cramped interior of the capsule. There was barely room for the two of them, and what room there was had been designed to seat creatures with wriggly things for legs. Aliens crowded around the launch tube, peering in at them, their eyes sliding around for a better look.

"Activate something!" said Patsy. "Get us out of here!"

Detecting their presence, the capsule's command system suddenly came on, lighting up the flight control panels. "Translation mode on," it said, peacefully. "Thank you for choosing Escape-O-Pod. Fee for use will be 200 credits, payable at the end of your flight."

Jeremy slapped his fist on the big red button marked LAUNCH.

"Oh goody, something to eat," said Patsy.

"Launch," tutted Jeremy, "not lunch."

In an instant, they were squashed to the back of the capsule as it fired like a bullet up the launch tube and out into the Martian atmosphere. Suddenly, there was wide open space all around. Their stomachs did a couple of somersaults, decided that was a bad idea and shrunk down towards their feet instead.

"Yeeeehaaaa!" cried Patsy.

"I don't feel well," cried Jeremy.

About a dozen other capsules were being launched right behind them. The aliens at the controls had been specially trained for space combat, and had all spent many hours learning to fly their machines.

Jeremy and Patsy hadn't.

"They're gaining on us!" said Patsy, watching the large tactical display which had blinked into life next to her left ear.

"They wouldn't be chasing us if they couldn't bring us down," reasoned Jeremy. "They're probably armed."

Glowing, round energy bolts exploded against the outside of the capsule. It rocked and dipped wildly. More bolts flew past them, scorching the capsule's casing and windows.

"Why do I always have to be right?" Jeremy wailed. Then he turned to the flight controls. "Command system, do you understand me?"

"Translation mode on," said the command system, even more peacefully than before.

"Evasive manoeuvres!" said Jeremy.

"Optional evasive manoeuvres program is available at an additional charge of 500 credits."

"Do it!" said Jeremy. "And switch on whatever ray guns we've got!"

"Thank you," said the command system. "U-Blast-Em torpedoes supplied at 45 credits per unit."

A bulky pair of joysticks hummed into view next to Patsy, alongside a display showing targeting information. She flipped the safety cover off the FIRE button.

"Cool," she grinned.

The capsule ducked and dived as the evasive manoeuvres program switched itself on. Jeremy and Patsy were squashed from one side to another and back again. Through the windows, the red mountains of Mars seemed to whirl and twist ahead of them.

Patsy let rip with a volley of torpedoes every time one of their pursuers came in range. She didn't actually hit anything, but she had loads of fun trying.

The aliens' capsules buzzed and whizzed. Their carefully aimed shots were rapidly destroying the outer casing of Jeremy and Patsy's craft. Warning lights kept coming on all over the flight controls.

"Vital systems damaged," said the command system as peacefully as it was possible to say it. "Destruction likely. Thank you for your custom."

"We've got to get back to the alien base or we'll be blown to bits," said Jeremy.

"Oh, let's take one of these capsules, Patsy, he says," grumbled Patsy. "Let's escape, he says. Thanks a heap! I get tested on French grammar AND blown to bits on the same day!"

Jeremy ignored her. "Got to think of a way to get us back," he muttered.

The capsule shook violently as another barrage of bolts pounded it. Parts of the engine vaporised, and showers of hull fragments exploded all over the place. Then the capsule spun rapidly as a small hole was blasted in its main window. Air began to rush out.

The evasive manoeuvres program decided the situation was hopeless, and erased itself. Now the capsule was hurtling along in a straight line which would take it out into the depths of space.

Jeremy reckoned his brain had

erased itself too.

"Wait," said Patsy. "I know a way to turn the capsule around and return to the alien base!"

"Patsy, you're a marvel!" cried Jeremy. "Have you worked out a way to bypass the flight control systems?"

"No, there's a button here marked RETURN TO BASE."

She pressed it.

The capsule whirled upwards, round and back the way it had come, at a speed which left Jeremy and Patsy trying very hard not to think of greasy food. The pursuing aliens didn't have time to react before it was out of their firing range.

As they neared the alien base, Jeremy noticed something which would turn out to be important when they reached Chapter Three.

The capsule shot back down its launch tube, and into the loading bay. It skidded to a halt at the end of the corridor along which our heroes had been chased, and steamed quietly to itself.

"Total bill for usage and repairs is 134,241 credits," coughed the command system weakly. "Please place payment in the slot marked PAYMENT. Any recognised galactic currency is acceptable. We look forward to your next escape flight with us."

"What?" cried Patsy. "We haven't got any recognised galactic currency!"

Jeremy pulled his French exercise book from his pocket, ripped out the pages, and stuffed them into the slot. The capsule's accounting system had been badly damaged, and mistook them for Plutonian dollars. The door's locking clamps unhooked themselves with a hiss.

Jeremy and Patsy kicked open the door and tumbled out. Aliens were already appearing from the other end of the docking bay, rippling towards them on their tentacles. Without a word, Patsy hauled Jeremy to his feet and they ran back down the corridor as fast as their shaky legs and even shakier stomachs would take them.

The corridor was clear, but the control room was back to being fully manned. Well, fully aliened. The aliens all turned at the same time and, adjusting their translators, hurried forward to intercept.

"Earthlings are prohibited by Order 563, Article B!"

"Failure to comply will result in a term of imprisonment!"

"Failure to halt is not in line with accepted procedure!"

They rushed at them, eye-stalks and tentacles waving.

"Hurry!" called Patsy. Jeremy quickly placed his hand on the door of the transport portal. As soon as it was open wide enough to step through, Patsy pushed him into the vortex.

"See ya!" she called to the aliens, jumping in herself, as tentacles swung out to grab her legs. The door hummed shut.

CHAPTER THREE

**In which Earth's defences are neutralised,
and Patsy gets really, really hungry**

On Earth, the woods were reassuringly full of twittering birds and burrowing moles. Frankly, Jeremy and Patsy wouldn't have cared if the moles had been twittering and the birds burrowing, they were just glad to be back on a familiar planet. They glanced at the closed portal behind them. It stayed shut.

"I don't think they're going to follow us," gasped Jeremy, trying to catch his breath. They set off wearily, out of the woods.

"Maybe they can't survive in our atmosphere?" said Patsy.

"No, we were OK on their base, remember. They breath air like we do. Which means they're not from Mars themselves, because Mars doesn't have an atmosphere like ours." Jeremy combed his hair, while he thought about the situation. "I don't think they want to be seen on Earth. Not yet."

"Why?" said Patsy.

"Well, look at them. They'd have real trouble trying to dress up as humans and blend in. They're keeping their distance until their plans are more advanced."

"So how did this transporter door thing get here?"

"Elementary, my dear Patsy," said Jeremy. "They're being helped."

If the two of them had been characters in a movie, this would have been the perfect point for a DAN-DAN-DAAAA bit. But they weren't. Instead, Jeremy made an observation, based on his reading of the MI7 booklet 'Dangerous Gadgets At A Glance':

"When we were in the escape capsule, on the way back to the base, did you notice something?" (This is the something mentioned in the last chapter).

"What sort of something?" said Patsy.

"A sort of enormous cannon-type something that could easily have been the device used to fire the energy beam which destroyed the university?"

"No, I didn't," said Patsy.

"Lucky I did, then," said Jeremy. "And if the beam was fired from Mars, I bet it needed a homing beacon to reach its target accurately. Which means somebody placed one."

"Which confirms they're being helped," concluded Patsy.

"Hmm," said Jeremy. "The plot is thickening faster than school gravy."

He was right. Back at their Martian base, the aliens had done three important things:

1. Cleaned up the mess left by Jeremy and Patsy.

2. Brought forward their attack plans, because Jeremy and Patsy had found their base and would now try to foil their evil schemes.

3. Put on their blue combat shirts. These combat shirts were covered in disgustingly rude insults, written in twenty-seven galactic languages, so that the aliens could be nasty to as many beings as possible, all in one go.

In the control room, the aliens' leader, distinguishable by the floppy Hat Of Grandness he wore, settled into his squidgy throne behind his electronic campaign desk. This was Gruntox The Big. At his side stood his second in command, Dungsit The Many Tentacled. Their words are shown here in translation:

"As advised by Section B of the Destruction Of Earth Act," grunted Gruntox, "move the scoopotron out of hiding place D and into position 1!"

"Aye aye, Your Bigness!" Dungsit saluted with four of his many tentacles.

"And don't muck it up, Dungsit!" grunted Gruntox.

"No no, Your Bigness!"

Dungsit rippled over to a mobile control unit, and wrapped tentacles around two fat levers which jutted out at the front. Above the levers was a screen, and on the screen could be seen the Earth, and the Moon...

On the dark side on the Moon, hidden well out of sight, the scoopotron floated gently in space. It was the size of six football pitches, but wasn't nearly as green. Out of one end unwound what looked like an immensely long, fat hose.

As Dungsit pushed and pulled levers back on Mars, the scoopotron's engines powered up. It glided gracefully out of the Moon's shadow, and headed down towards the surface of the Earth... towards the northern hemisphere... towards Europe...

In dozens of tracking stations, situated in dozens of countries, the scoopotron appeared as an enormous blip on radar screens, alongside a tiny marker saying LOOK OUT! IT'S A MENACING ALIEN WAR MACHINE!

The people at these tracking stations weren't sure what to do. First, they ran up and down and cried for their mums. Then, they had some sweeties and an ice cream, and that made them feel better. Finally, they launched every missile and fighter aircraft they had.

A wave of weaponry closed in on the alien invader...

"Wave of weaponry closing in!" called Gruntox's third in command, Podclone The Fat, from a console at the other end of the control room.

Gruntox turned to Dungsit. "Procedure 158, Amendment 2!" he growled.

"Aye aye, Your Bigness!" saluted Dungsit. He pulled more levers.

"And make sure you pull the right ones, Dungsit!" growled Gruntox.

"Aye aye, Your Bigness!"

"Wave of weaponry neutralised!" called Podclone a few moments later. "Offensive material has been pushed back to ground level! Cost of attack holding steady at 200,000 credits!"

Gruntox grinned horribly to

himself. How he loved pulverising little planets, and how he loved doing it without having to spend a fortune. "Soon it will be ours," he dribbled. "All of it. Billions and trillions of credits' worth." He started giggling sneakily behind a couple of tentacles.

All the other aliens in the control room started giggling too. Gruntox's fourth in command, Mary The Stupidly Named, pulled himself together enough to make his report: "Our Earth agent has completed form T216, Your Bigness, to inform you that the next homing beacon will soon be in place, at Target 2..."

At Grotside School, the bell rang for lunchtime. It didn't ring for long, because it always got smacked with a hockey stick.

The corridors and stairways were suddenly crammed with people rushing in opposite directions. The more daring and reckless pupils were heading for the Dining Hall. The more sensible and health-conscious ones were steering well clear of the Dining Hall, and heading off home or into town for lunch. The teachers were making a dash for the Staff Room, where they could sit and drink coffee, mumble fearfully to themselves, and try to steady their trembling nerves ready for the afternoon.

Amid the confusion and the clouds of chalk dust, a mysterious figure walked almost un-noticed. The figure carried a black bag. To one side of the school's entrance hall, which was slap bang in the middle of the main building, the figure stopped, crouched, and unzipped the bag.

From inside was lifted a sleek, metallic device. The figure held it delicately against the nearest wall. Small grippers suddenly sprang out from around its base, and dug hard into the concrete. An antenna whirred upwards from its top, and at the tip of the antenna flashed a tiny red light. The homing beacon began to emit a regular *bip-bip-bip-bip*, as the figure hurried away...

Meanwhile, Jeremy was coming to a conclusion.

"...So in conclusion," he said, "I reckon that the aliens' agent on Earth is likely to be someone from the university itself. It would be an ideal first target, you see, because the agent wouldn't have to get into some strange building, where any number of alarms might be set off."

Patsy was humming quietly to herself, with her fingers in her ears. Jeremy hadn't noticed.

"Which means," he continued, "that the aliens weren't trying to destroy the university as such. They just wanted to destroy something convenient. Which also means that... Patsy, are you listening?"

"No."

Jeremy sulked all the way back to the enormous pile of rubble that had once been the university. Professor

Killjoy, Dr Nicely and Mr Smith were sitting on crumpled bits of filing cabinet, tucking into a posh-looking hamper of food.

"Splendid!" shouted the Professor, gobbling down half a pork pie. "Excellent!"

Dr Nicely waved at Jeremy, and he blushed yet again. "Do join us," she said. "Just something I threw together from a few leftovers at home. Salad with vinegar dressing, mushroom and kiwi fruit vol au vents, lobster with spicy Mexican salsa dip..."

"Got any chips?" said Patsy.

Jeremy perched next to Dr Nicely, and picked up a slice of broccoli quiche. "Thanks ever so much," he said with a soppy grin.

Mr Smith nibbled at a cream cracker. Patsy pulled a face at the taste of the spicy Mexican salsa dip.

"Are your investigations progressing, Mr Brown?" said Dr Nicely, her eyelashes batting gently at him.

"We've made some significant

discoveries, Dr Nicely, thank you for asking," said Jeremy. "Although they are, I'm afraid, rather disturbing and terrifying."

"We're all gonna be killed by aliens," said Patsy through a mouthful of garlic sausage. She pulled another face and spat the sausage out into a paper napkin.

"Aliens!" shouted the Professor. "Rubbish!"

"The existence of life in other parts of the galaxy has yet to be proved," said Mr Smith.

"I'm sure someone as charming as Mr Brown wouldn't make up a story like that," said Dr Nicely.

"I'm not listening to some lah-de-dah MI7 twaddle!" shouted the Professor.

"You never know, perhaps the aliens are in league with the Loch Ness Monster," said Mr Smith dryly, pushing his tiny round glasses back up to the top of his nose.

"I'm afraid that they ARE in league

with someone on Earth," said Jeremy, trying to sound dramatic and exciting, and yet at the same time confident and reassuring.

"Yeah, it's one of you lot," said Patsy. She bit into an onion flan, pulled another face, and flung the rest of it over her shoulder.

"One of us?" yelled the Professor. "Piffle!"

"Perhaps one of us IS the Loch Ness Monster," droned Mr Smith.

"Are you quite sure?" said Dr Nicely. One of her neat eyebrows arched elegantly.

"Yes," said Jeremy, blushing all over again. "But don't worry. I'm on the case. I once saved a train by swallowing the miniature timer on a three tonne bomb."

"Then he puked it up out of the window," said Patsy.

"Thank you, Patsy," said Jeremy through gritted teeth. "Any other intellectual gems you'd like to add to the conversation?"

Patsy was now feeling really, really hungry. She nearly said "Yes, let's go and get some chips before the shop shuts," but instead she pointed to an object she'd spotted in the sky. An object with a long hose-thing snaking out in front of it.

"What's that?" she cried.

"Ah!" shouted the Professor. "That'll be the men from the council, come to start clearing away all this rubble!"

The scoopotron descended at the about the same speed as Jeremy's and Patsy's jaws. Its engines rose to a howling roar. The hose, about the width of the Channel Tunnel, dipped towards the rubble. With a rumbling clatter, lumps of concrete began to be sucked up.

The humans crawled away as fast as they could manage. The suction pulled hard on their clothes and hair. The remains of the picnic splattered and bounced over the debris, and shot up into the machine with a slurp.

"They only had to send a lorry!" yelled the Professor.

"That's not from the council!" yelled Dr Nicely. "That's from another planet!"

The five humans scattered, gradually finding movement easier as they got further away from the scoopotron. Jeremy and Patsy took cover behind a post box.

"They want the building itself!" cried Patsy.

"They must have brought their plans forward, letting that thing out in the open so soon!" cried Jeremy. "But if all it does is suck up concrete, it won't have much to keep itself occupied with. Unless there's about to be a second target!"

"Such as?"

"Don't know," muttered Jeremy thoughtfully. "Just here there's only the woods, and the university, and... the school! Patsy, they're going to destroy the school!"

"Yipee!"

"Patsy! People could get hurt! The aliens' agent must have planted a homing beacon somewhere in the school buildings. We've got to deactivate it before it's—"

Too late. A weird humming spread out across the area, even louder than the sound of the scoopotron. The air itself seemed to shake and blur. Helplessly, Jeremy and Patsy watched as a fat red beam of energy flashed vertically from the sky.

The school playing fields erupted, shooting mud and grass hundreds of metres into the air. Violent tremors knocked Jeremy and Patsy off their feet.

"They're closing in!" Patsy cried.

CHAPTER FOUR

**In which our heroes risk life and limb,
and get no thanks for it at all**

"Thank goodness it's lunchtime," said Jeremy. "Half the buildings are empty."

A second energy beam flashed into the school swimming pool. The pool vaporised in a cloud of high-pressure steam.

"Quick!" cried Patsy. "We've got to find that beacon!"

They ran to the school, bent double as if ducking out of the way of something. It was a pointless thing to do, because nothing could have stopped them being disintegrated if a beam had actually hit them. But they did it anyway.

The weird humming sound was building up all around them again. Another blast was seconds away. They hurtled into the entrance hall of the main school building, and slid to a halt on the highly polished floor.

"Oi!" came a grumpy voice from behind them. "I just finished shining that!" Mr Vim, the school caretaker, bustled towards them. His black moustache was as bristly as his broom, and his brown overalls were dotted with old paint stains.

"There!" cried Patsy, spotting the beacon clamped to the wall. They hurried over to it.

"Thank goodness the aliens' agent has no imagination," said Jeremy. "Or we might never have found it." He set to work examining the device.

"Oi!" barked Mr Vim. "I said I just finished shining that floor! Look at the marks you've put on it!"

"I'm really sorry, Mr Vim," said Jeremy, "but the whole school's about to explode. Please excuse me." He searched around the beacon's casing for a control panel. At one end was a touch sensor. He pressed it and a little hatch flipped open, revealing a set of buttons with alien symbols on them.

"An hour and a half I spent doing that, you young thug," grumbled Mr Vim. "I'm going to report you!"

Outside, the humming in the sky reached a note that the school choir had been searching for since Christmas. A red flash suddenly slammed into the far end of the Modern Languages block. Half the building instantly shattered with a deafening BANG.

Fortunately, the far end of the Modern Languages block hadn't contained a single pupil. Unfortunately, it HAD contained the Staff Room and the Headmaster's private study. As the building exploded, twenty-eight screaming teachers were shot high into the sky. Almost all of them spilled their coffee.

Fortunately, none of them sustained serious damage: seven (including Madame Croissant) landed in nearby trees; eleven made teacher-shaped holes in other buildings; eight were flipped onto the roof of the gym; one would have had a soft landing if the swimming pool had still contained water.

The Headmaster was shot across the mess that had now replaced the playing fields, and slithered to a stop in a muddy trench. The copy of *Fluffy Bunnybears Monthly* he'd been happily reading in his study had burnt away to little crispy bits.

Meanwhile, Jeremy was determined to deactivate the beacon using logical reasoning and the application of intelligent thought. He had no idea where to begin.

"Let's just smash it!" cried Patsy. "The next shot could hit US!"

"Patsy," said Jeremy, "there's no need to resort to mindless violence."

"I'm going to get a mop and a bucket!" grumbled Mr Vim. "You can clean off those marks yourselves!"

The walls around them suddenly

buckled and split. A thunderous rumble of dust and smoke billowed through the hall. Mr Vim, clutching his broom tightly, was blown out of the building like a cork from a bottle.

"So much for being sensible," wailed Jeremy. "Smash it!"

With one flying kick from Patsy, the beacon was in pieces.

And so was half the main building. Another blast pulverised six classrooms and a toilet block.

"It's made no difference!" yelled Jeremy. "Their targeting systems must have a firm lock on the school. There's only one thing for it now, Patsy. We've got to go back to Mars and shut the whole thing down!"

"Oh great," moaned Patsy. "Another chance to risk life and limb. Hurray."

"Patsy," said Jeremy grandly, "it is our duty and our privilege to fight evil, even if it means facing horrible dangers and getting all grubby. Now come on."

Ducking pieces of flying school

and scrambling past mounds of classroom, they headed for the portal in the woods. They kept well clear of the scoopotron, which was still busy sucking up lumps of concrete. Behind them, the humming noise was rising again.

They hurried along the muddy path between the trees and bushes.

"What's that vacuum machine thing doing?" said Patsy.

"The best person to tell us has to be the aliens' agent," said Jeremy.

"And the aliens' agent has to be Dr Nicely!"

"Don't be silly," said Jeremy, "she wouldn't hurt a fly, let alone betray her entire planet to a bunch of intergalactic tentacled monsters! It's clearly Professor Killjoy."

"Oh yeah? Nicely knew it was an energy beam that had blown up the university! AND she was the one who suggested searching these woods! AND she pointed out that vacuum machine thing is alien!"

"She's simply a highly intelligent person," said Jeremy, blushing just ever so slightly. "Witty and refined. We have a lot in common. Besides, if it was her she'd try to throw us off the scent, not reveal things that are true. No, mark my words, Killjoy's the villain."

"Why?"

"He's a right misery, that's why."

They came to a sudden halt. The portal's door was already open. Through it they could see the swirling vortex that led to the aliens' Martian base.

"I think we're about to find out, one way or the other," said Jeremy. "Looks like their agent has just this minute gone through!"

Pausing only to give each other a quick 'oh crumbs' look, they stepped into the vortex themselves.

In the Martian control room, Gruntox and the rest of the aliens were getting so excited they were beginning to wobble up and down in their seats.

"Concrete!" gurgled Gruntox, his tentacles wriggling. "Lovely concrete!"

"We love concrete!" chorused the other aliens. Then they giggled a bit.

A humanoid figure, their agent on Earth, watched them from the shadows, smiling an evil, greedy smile.

"Scoopotron now in position C12!" said Dungsit, pulling levers on the scoopotron's control unit. "Scoopotron belly now holding 567.9 mega-loads, Your Bigness!"

"Lovely, lovely," gurgled Gruntox. "Don't muck it up, Dungsit, steady as she goes."

"Aye aye, sir!"

"Zap-O-Matic energy beam ready to fire again, Your Bigness!" called Podclone. Two of his tentacles were poised over the button that would launch another attack on the school.

"Wait!"

Jeremy's voice was as loud and commanding as he could make it. The aliens' eyes swivelled around on their stalks and glared at him. Jeremy had adopted a heroic, arms folded, legs apart stance (which he'd learnt from volume three of the MI7 manual 'Be Cool With Body Posture'), in order to show the aliens he meant business. Patsy just made rude signs at them.

"Humans are illegal!" grizzled Gruntox into his translator. "Interference is illegal! Seize them in accordance with the Grabbing Of Prisoners Act!"

Half a dozen aliens slithered over and wrapped tentacles tightly around Jeremy's and Patsy's arms. They were dragged over to Gruntox's throne. Patsy struggled like mad.

"Don't fight them, Patsy," said Jeremy. "We're here to talk." He turned to Gruntox. Now he had a chance to actually speak to the aliens, he wasn't really sure what to say to them. "Look, just stop all this nonsense, OK?"

"Yeah, game over, Ugly," said Patsy.

Gruntox called up a string of symbols on his control screen. "These two humans are in violation of 226 separate regulations. They have an unpaid escape pod bill, which they attempted to settle using forged Plutonian dollars! They will be held in prison until they hand over enough credits to pay for their trial!"

"Why not simply throw them outside?" said a cold, calm voice from the shadows. "They wouldn't last two minutes in the Martian atmosphere. Then we'd be rid of them."

"That would be the cheapest option, Your Bigness," called Podclone, tapping at a calculator.

Patsy screwed up her eyes in an effort to see who the aliens' agent was. She needn't have bothered, because at that moment the thin, grey figure of the lab assistant, Mr Smith, stepped forward into a pool of light beside Gruntox's throne.

"I KNEW it wasn't Dr Nicely," said Jeremy.

"I leave their fate in your tentacles, Your Bigness," said Mr Smith. "The invasion must continue. Give me more beacons, and I'll return to Earth and prepare more targets."

"Why are you doing this, Smith?" said Jeremy. "And who are these aliens?"

Mr Smith pushed his little, round glasses back to the top of his nose. His flat, dull smile made even Gruntox shiver. "I made contact through my work at the university. I picked up a random subspace transmission, and answered it. Gruntox The Big and his business partners here roam the Galaxy in search of—"

"Concrete," gurgled Gruntox, "lovely concrete. Beeaaauuuuutiful."

"It's very rare and precious in many parts of space," said Mr Smith. "I led them to our unprofitable little planet, which of course is positively covered in it. I'm helping them take control of Earth."

"And in return," said Jeremy, "they're giving you loads of—"

"Money," gurgled Mr Smith, "lovely

money. Beeaaauuuuutiful. Gruntox and I can't exactly wear each other's combat shirts, but we're still two of a kind."

Gruntox and the other aliens giggled behind their tentacles in a way which Patsy thought rather silly and childish. Mr Smith operated a set of controls by Gruntox's throne, and a huge bag full of homing beacons came up through a hatch in the floor. He heaved the bag onto his shoulder.

"Goodbye, Mr Brown. Goodbye, Miss Spudd. Why not start trade talks with the aliens? You never know, you might be able to sell them your garden patio for a few credits. Before they come and take it, ha, ha, ha, ha."

Jeremy had a sudden idea, and he often found that ideas which turned up suddenly were the best ones.

"Good!" he said loudly, so that the entire control room could hear him. "Can't wait to be rid of it. Full of concrete-worm, it is. Falling apart."

"Eh?" said Mr Smith.

Gruntox fumbled hurriedly with

his translator, to make sure it was working properly. "The human will repeat himself by order of Rule 55!"

"Of course!" cried Jeremy, even louder. "I said our concrete at home has got concrete-worm. Right through it. It's falling to bits."

Patsy caught on to what he was up to. She started giggling in a way which the aliens thought rather silly and childish. Gruntox came over all faint and dizzy.

"The human will explain concrete-worm!" he gibbered. "What does it do to l-l-lovely concrete?"

"Don't listen to him!" cried Mr Smith. "He's lying! He's jealous of our deal!"

"Concrete worm, or *Nastius Chewemupius* to give it its full name, is a tiny, burrowing insect," proclaimed Jeremy. "It lays little pink eggs in deep holes in any concrete structure. These eggs hatch, and the furry things with teeth that come out eat all the concrete around them."

The aliens shivered with disgust. Some of them wrapped shaking tentacles around their mouths to stop themselves being sick.

"Ignore him!" screamed Mr Smith. "He's just trying to rob me of my money!"

"They're a constant problem," continued Jeremy. All the aliens gasped. "Humans spend billions of credits every year fumigating buildings." Several aliens wet their combat shirts. "We humans have to keep painting over our concrete with washing up liquid and milk to protect it..." The aliens who didn't squeal with horror ran straight for the toilets.

"Why didn't you warn us of this, Smith?" gargled Gruntox, trying not to cry.

"Because it's NOT TRUE!" screeched Mr Smith, his face turning from grey to purple.

"Oh now, be fair, Mr Smith," said Jeremy. "You wanted these poor aliens' money. Of course you weren't going to tell them about concrete-worm." He turned to Gruntox. "That makes sense, doesn't it, Your Bigness?"

Gruntox nodded, stuffing a hanky into his mouth.

"We came here to put you in the picture, didn't we Patsy?" said Jeremy. "I mean, Earthlings are fair and honest. We couldn't let you have contaminated concrete. Wouldn't be good for business."

"C-C-Contaminated," gurgled Gruntox, sobbing.

Podclone tapped hurriedly at his calculator. "Costs of decontamination are... are... are beyond calculation, Your Bigness!" he wailed.

"Of course, there's galloping sand-rot in most concrete too," added Jeremy.

Gruntox pulled himself together, and stood up.

"Invasion is cancelled, in line with Emergency Planning Procedures! This base is to be recycled! Humans will be ejected!"

CHAPTER FIVE

**In which the aliens stick to the rules,
and Jeremy sticks to the floor**

"Ejected?" howled Mr Smith. "After all I've done for you?"

Podclone rippled over to Gruntox clutching a thick wad of papers, and whispered something while pointing to a tiny, printed footnote on the last sheet. Gruntox nodded, and turned to Mr Smith.

"Not ejected, Smith," he growled. Mr Smith gasped with relief. "Sold!" grunted Gruntox. Mr Smith gasped with horror.

"What?" he yelled.

"Paragraph 9, Subsection 34, Condition 12 of your contract clearly states that your body and all its contents become our property if invasion plans are called off at any time for any reason in any way! Those are the rules! You will work for 20 years in the Invoicing Department on Andromeda - without pay! Take him away!"

Mr Smith turned to Jeremy and Patsy. "This is your fault!" he hissed evilly. He just had time to press a button on a nearby console, before a dozen aliens surrounded him and dragged him out of the control room. He was too busy kicking and screaming to say anything else.

"They don't mess about, this lot, do they?" whispered Patsy.

"That's what I'm afraid of," whispered Jeremy, watching Gruntox ordering buttons to be pushed and levers to be pulled.

The control room lights began to dim. Everything in the room seemed to blur and... slide? Gruntox spoke into a microphone on a flexible stalk, which he pulled out of the arm of his throne. His voice filled the entire area:

"This station will now melt down to its basic molecules! Recycling will then begin! Invasion force will withdraw and regroup! All staff and business partners to escape pods! Everyone to escape pods!"

"What about us?" called Patsy.

"Humans will be ejected," growled Gruntox.

"Since we helped you out," said Jeremy quickly, "why not let us use the transporter door thing, and go home?"

Gruntox thought for a moment. The ceiling was starting to drip and run down the walls, and the walls were starting to run across the floor.

"Very well," he grumbled, reluctantly. "I am merciful."

With that, he hurried off towards the escape pods, followed closely by all the other aliens. The lights grew dimmer. Control consoles and display screens began to sag lazily.

"Better hurry," said Jeremy.

He placed a hand on the transporter portal's operating panel. The door slid back, but the vortex beyond it was dim and patchy, nothing like it had been before.

"No power!" cried Jeremy helplessly. "We won't get through! Or we might get through, but it'll dump us in space!" Then he remembered something. "Smith! That was what he did at the controls, before they dragged him away. The rotten low-life switched off the power!"

"So this is it," said Patsy, "we end up melted into nothing, millions of miles from home."

"Chin up, Patsy," said Jeremy, whose chin was pretty down at that moment. "There must be a way out of this. Did I ever tell you about the time I foiled a bank robbery with two walnuts and a bag of crisps?"

"Yes."

The control room continued to fold in on itself like a slowly deflating balloon. Machines were gradually melting together into pools of alien metals and plastics. One of the controls that had already dissolved into nothing was the one to turn the portal's power back on.

"What have we got?" mumbled Jeremy to himself. "What can we use?"

"Think of something!" shouted Patsy. "Before ALL the controls are gone!"

Jeremy tried to run over to the remaining consoles, but found that his feet had sunk into the floor, which was rapidly turning into a sticky, squishy goo. "You'll have to operate it, Patsy! Quick, over there!"

"Operate what?" cried Patsy, jumping out of the way of a sudden floorslide. She dashed over to where Dungsit had been standing.

"There, next to you!" called Jeremy. "That screen shows a pile of school. Those must be the controls for that vacuum machine on Earth."

"So?"

"So drive it into the woods, and point it at the other transporter door thing! The suction might pull us clear from this end!"

Back on Earth, the scoopotron

suddenly lurched backwards as Patsy yanked its control levers on Mars. It rose and fell in the air, and made noises like half a dozen cows trapped in a falling elevator. It spun, sending its long nozzle flapping wildly, before zooming off in a zig-zag.

A battered and smoke-damaged huddle of teachers from Grotside School had collected on the edge of the woods. They spoke softly to each other, and took turns wiping mud off the Headmaster.

Here they were safe from exploding school buildings. What they weren't safe from was the scoopotron. It leapt into view over the trees, and with a flying twirl swatted them with its nozzle. They found themselves hurled into the air for the second time that day, but none of them could be bothered to scream this time.

"Haven't you got the hang of it yet, Patsy?"

"Allright, allright, I'm doing my

best!" Patsy pulled and pushed at the scoopotron's controls. "There! I worked out how to dump the stuff that was already inside it!"

The scoopotron zig-zagged into the woods, leaving the teachers to dig themselves free of the many tonnes of concrete that were now on top of them. It crashed into trees and vacuumed up squirrels.

Finally, the portal was in sight. Its door was open, and the pale, powerless vortex stirred groggily beyond. The scoopotron swung around for a few moments, then settled into position about fifty metres away. It's nozzle snaked unsteadily in front of it.

"I see it!" called Patsy. "I can see the transporter thing!"

At that moment, the ceiling of the control room flopped sideways. A gaping hole opened up above them. Out through the hole swirled the control room's air. In through the hole swirled the red dust of the Martian plains.

"Now!" yelled Jeremy. "Switch the vacuum on!"

Patsy pulled a lever, which collapsed into mush in her hand. As the scoopotron started up on Earth, a powerful suction pulled at the portal in the woods, through the interplanetary vortex, and into the control room. Jeremy's shoes were tugged free of the melted floor with a plop, and he shot into the vortex. Patsy, feeling the pull of the scoopotron, simply jumped up and let it yank her through.

The control room, and the rest of the aliens' base, shrank away into wobbly mounds of different coloured goo, which waited patiently for a recycling ship to pick them up.

Jeremy and Patsy whizzed through the vortex and out of the portal in the woods. They dug their fingers into the grass and held on tight, to avoid being swallowed up by the scoopotron. The suction set their school uniforms flapping like washing hung out to dry in a hurricane. Their fingers slipped as the ground beneath them trembled.

But within moments, the force that was pulling at them subsided. Now that its controls on Mars had melted away, the scoopotron was beginning to drift. It rose and floated aimlessly above the trees. Its suction mechanism switched off, and the whine of its engines wound down.

The portal closed and locked itself. It bleeped twice, and then it too began to drift up above the trees. Both machines slowly moved off, and dwindled to weeny dots. And then they were gone.

Jeremy's voice broke the silence: "I think the aliens have recalled them to Mars."

Patsy sat up and smeared the grass from her hands down her blazer. "I'm starving," she said. "Now can we go to the chip shop?"

Pausing only for Jeremy to complain about how the melting floor had completely ruined his shoes, they set off to find Professor Killjoy and Dr Nicely (to tell them they'd need to find a new lab assistant). They thought they'd avoid the school for the time being, since about a third of it was lying in ruins, and the teachers wouldn't be in the best of moods.

"When I write this up in my memoirs," said Jeremy, adjusting his tie, "I'll call the chapter 'How I Saved The Whole Of The Earth From Certain Demolition.'"

Patsy made a remark about Jeremy's memoirs that can't be repeated, but Jeremy wasn't listening. He could feel a sharp buzzing sensation in his completely ruined shoes.

THE END

ABOUT THE AUTHOR

Simon Cheshire is the author of many hugely popular books for children and teenagers, including the bestselling Saxby Smart detective stories. He writes in a tiny little office, which used to be a cupboard, and which is bursting at the seams with books, old chocolate wrappers and letters from his readers. He writes using an Apple Mac and a mug of coffee. Many of his best ideas come to him while he's staring out of the window. He lives in Warwick, but spends most of his time in a world of his own.

Also available

They Melted His Brain!
Totally Unsuitable For Children
Bottomby

Saxby Smart: Private Detective series
The Curse of the Ancient Mask
The Fangs of the Dragon
The Pirate's Blood
The Hangman's Lair
The Eye Of The Serpent
Five Seconds To Doomsday
The Poisoned Arrow
Secret Of The Skull

SIMON CHESHIRE
WWW.SIMONCHESHIRE.CO.UK

Lightning Source UK Ltd.
Milton Keynes UK
. 27 April 2010
153355UK00001B/80/P